Chasing Wildflowers

Chasing Wildflowers

.....

*A Mad
Search for Wild
Gardens*

.....

SCOTT CALHOUN

RIO NUEVO PUBLISHERS
TUCSON, ARIZONA

Contents

Preface

Hitting the Wildflower Highway

· · · · · · · · · · · · · ·

BEGINNING IN THE NOW FAMOUSLY wet spring of 2005 and through the drought into the wet summer of 2006, I took a series of trips around the Southwest to find wildflowers. I left my home in Tucson and followed a blooming river of flowers from northwestern Mexico, to southern California, up to Utah, across Colorado, down through New Mexico, and over to west Texas. Once I hit the wildflower highway, I found that I had a hard time stopping. I discovered that I had an unlimited appetite for intricate wild landscapes. These trips profoundly informed my little garden-design practice. Several times—after photographing pink dunes covered with Kanab yucca (*Yucca kanabensis*) and rough mules ears (*Wyethia scabra*)

in southern Utah, and finding a clump of Parry's primrose (*Primula parryi*) below a snowfield-and-granite peak in the Colorado Rockies—I questioned whether I could ever design a garden again.

The odd thing was I found the converse to be true. After returning from each wildflower-hunting trip, I approached my garden-design work with renewed vigor—inspired by what I had seen. Hundreds of little wild-garden templates filled my head, just waiting for the right situation to use them in. I would open up my laptop, look at a photo of black volcanic rock covered in purple mat (*Nama hispidum*), brittlebush (*Encelia farinosa*),

Firewheel along a Texas roadside just outside Fredericksburg.

senita cactus (*Lophocereus schottii*), and ironwood trees (*Olneya tesota*), and ask, "Could this idea work in the Andersens' garden?" All of the best characteristics of dry gardens were exhibited in wild landscapes: interesting geology, bold forms, repetition, and drought tolerance. By looking at the exposure, soil types, and moisture requirements of the wild plants I saw, I could amend and improve my plant palette and have more confidence about what would grow where.

I'm certainly not the first desert rat to go plant exploring in arid lands. I'm following in the footsteps of Howard Scott Gentry, Ron Gass, John Fairey, Carl Schoenfeld, Mark Dimmitt, Richard Felger, Matt Johnson, Janice Emily Bowers, Sean Hogan, Scott Odgen, and others. While my trips were considerably less scientific and taxonomically rigorous than the journeys of those botanizers, I did take pains to correctly identify and photograph the wild plants I encountered. That said, this book will not suss out minute differences between plants that require a magnifying glass to see. Like Everett Ruess, the legendary young California artist who disappeared for good in the Utah desert in 1934, I'm a "vagabond for beauty." My interest is in what is lovely in the wild, and what could be lovely in gardens.

These excursions have not been luxury junkets. With a small book advance, I drove my thrifty 1999 Jetta turbo diesel on most of these trips. I've slept in a combination of friends' homes, tents, cheap motels with dicey security, and occasionally my car. I had the pleasure of observing—and sometimes getting stuck in—dramatic weather patterns, like the massive late-spring storm that churned over the Antelope Valley Poppy Reserve in California while I hunkered down under a Joshua tree (*Yucca brevifolia*). I did eat well, and because the Southwest is full of cheap regional eats, a portion of the book is devoted to my road-food finds—like discovering what I believe to be the world's best fish tacos in Baja, Mexico, or rediscovering the joys of Utah shakes that you eat with a spoon. Because I'm lanky, with precious little fat in reserve, I need locally produced, high-fat nourishment to chase local wildflowers, because when I'm deprived of calories, I get surly.

One of the pleasures of wildflower hunting, besides the ontological delight of finding flowers, is the company. I've had the companionship of a poet, a hydro-geologist, a nationally known birder, a garden photographer, and several fellow garden designers. The great thing about cavorting with plant-heads is that on account of their enthusiasm for plants, they are poor secret-keepers. Because people know I'm looking for wildflowers, I get phone calls that begin with, "I saw this great stand of …" Without even asking, desert-plant guru and nursery owner Gene Joseph told me exactly how to find the largest boojum tree (*Fouquieria columnaris*) on the planet, and so began my search for the big boojum—a quest which, due to its phallic shape, invited many jokes about me compensating for something.

The past two years of chasing wildflowers has convinced me of three things: hiking boots are my best garden-design tool, there are many fine plants in the wild that are either undiscovered or ignored in mainstream horticulture, and lastly, the world of wild plants is full of kind and passionate people who will point you the way, walk with you, and sometimes take you by the hand, toward interesting plants. These are people who keep seed envelopes in their wallets, and they are here to help.

Why Chase Plants?

I could have chased golf balls across an emerald-green fairway or moneyed older women driving Jaguar coupes, but I settled on wildflowers. Maybe it's because their myriad constructions and colors never cease to fascinate me, or maybe because at thirty-nine—what feels like the equinox of my life—I don't want to waste another moment doing anything that diminishes my horizons. The trajectory of writing this book has taken me from a steady salaried nursery-management position to being a gleefully self-employed garden designer and garden writer. My life became more risky and more abundant. Like the Mexican gold poppy, I list toward the sun. My teenage daughter, Zoë, looks at me as though I'm crazy; my wife, Deirdre, maintains a practiced nonchalance.

The Geography of a Wildflower Adventure

When you look at a map of the Southwest, the political boundaries ignore the more important lines that delineate the great North American deserts: the Sonoran, the Mojave, the Chihuahuan, and the Great Basin. In writing this book, I focused much of my attention on these so-called "wastelands." My travels transported me to the dunes of northwest Sonora, Mexico, the sandstone-cathedral spires of Sedona, coral sands in southern Utah, the big valley of California, the sandy heart of Baja, the Chihuahuan desert of New Mexico and west Texas, and in an alpine mode, up into the thin air of the Wasatch Range and the Colorado Rockies. I finished up these journeys, in the fall of 2006, in the sky islands of southeast Arizona. I visited six U.S. states and the Mexican states of Sonora and Baja California Norte.

As is the custom in the U.S., each state has its own official flower. How they select just one is beyond me, but somehow each of these is in some way supposed to be emblematic.

- Arizona: the saguaro cactus blossom (*Carnegiea gigantea*)
- California: the California poppy (*Eschscholtzia californica*)
- Colorado: Colorado columbine (*Aquilegia caerulea*)
- New Mexico: soap tree yucca flower (*Yucca elata*)
- Texas: Texas bluebonnets (*Lupinus texensis*)
- Utah: sego lily (*Calochortus nuttallii*)

When I considered this list, I found it incredible and heartening that all of the flowers, except Colorado's, are desert plants, and even the yellow cousins of Colorado's famous pale-blue-and-white columbine creep into desert canyon habitat. With this in mind, I began my hunt, the search for my own garden-specific lists of flowers. I didn't have a checklist of really-must-see flowers, but I did want to be there at times when there was *something* to see; and with my eyes wide open, I was rarely disappointed.

Running for the Border: Pinacate

When: early March 2005
Destination: Highway 8 and Highway 2 in Sonora, Mexico
Total trip time: 28 hours
Vehicle: 1994 Honda Accord
Roundtrip distance from Tucson: 370 miles
Traveling companion: Simmons Buntin
Music: U2's The Joshua Tree

ON A SUNDAY MORNING in early March, I got up early to drink green tea and read my e-mail. Santa Fe-based photographer Charles Mann had sent me a message, as he does each spring, to inquire about the condition of wildflowers in Arizona. Charles, just returned from the California desert, wrote, "Sand verbena and primrose were fabulous at Imperial Dunes near El Centro about ten days ago—also at Anza Borrego. Please keep me posted on the wildflower news." We had been in the death grip of drought for the past five years, and until the winter of 2005 there wasn't much to report. In 2005, my rain gauge recorded over four inches of precipitation in January and February alone. On this dark morning, I considered the high likelihood of rivers of arroyo lupine (*Lupinus sparsiflorus*) on the sandy flats, and rocky hillsides of blazing Mexican gold poppies (*Eschscholtzia mexicana*), in Organ Pipe Cactus National Monument. I could almost feel it. If I kept working fifty-hour weeks at the nursery, I would surely miss the flower display of a lifetime. Logging on to the Arizona-Sonora Desert Museum's wildflower-watch website, I read the following post from Tucson horticulturists Gene Joseph and Jane Evans: "Pinacate Natural Park (Sonora): It's incredible. Drop everything and go NOW. Have never seen

Dunes south of Mexico Highway 2, rampant with desert sunflower, dune evening primrose, and sand verbena.

it so lush." There are some temptations that are too great for a renegade gardener to resist.

Calling mass desert-wildflower blooms "once-in-a-lifetime" events stretches the truth a little, but not much. Mark Dimmitt, the director of natural history at the Arizona–Sonora Desert Museum, writes that "In the six decades between 1940 and 1998, there have only been four documented drop-everything-and-go-see-it displays in southern Arizona: 1941, 1978, 1979, and 1998." If we count the seven decades since 1940, 2005 would make five such run-for-flowers events. "I have to go," I thought, "what if we have another thirty-seven-year wildflower drought like the one between 41 and 78—¡ay Chihuahua! I wouldn't be able to live with myself." I thought about something our beloved local radio horticulturist, Petey Mesquitey, said: "Spring is a short season in the desert; sometimes it only lasts two days—well, okay, maybe two weeks," and this compounded my sense of urgency.

I caught my friend—writer, editor, and environmental raconteur—Simmons Buntin, following a community meeting Sunday evening. "What are you doing the next couple of days?" I asked. "Working on *terrain.org* [the online magazine he edits]," he replied. "The new issue is coming out in two days." I knew Simmons was serious about getting his magazine out, but I also knew that as the editor-in-chief, he had, at various times in the past, postponed the release of the magazine, sometimes for something as insignificant as an Auburn University football game. At the same time, Simmons is not a one-dimensional sports guy; he is a poet and a part-time naturalist who, like me, is easily lured into the wild. "Simmons," I said, "we have a wildflower emergency."

By late Monday afternoon Simmons had called to say he was in and he could drive, and I miraculously rearranged my work schedule so I could be out for a little over a day. March was the busiest month of the year at the nursery; we had semi-trucks full of plants rolling in daily, and asking for a day off then might be met with hostility or derision from one's higher-ups. People would say to me, "It must be wonderful to work around all of these flowers," and it was—except on years when there were lots more flowers *outside* the nursery walls than within them. During springs like this, working in the nursery was agonizing. I used a song and dance, albeit one that I sincerely believed, about this year's wildflower bloom being a once- or maybe twice-in-a-lifetime event, etc., and to my astonishment my wildflower-vacation request was granted; I'd be out of the office—and out of the country—for a little over twenty-four hours.

We departed Tucson in Simmons's green 94 Honda Accord, with 150K miles on the odometer, on Tuesday morning—a clear, bright day with temperatures in the upper 70s. Both the trunk and the back seat were packed with an assortment of tents, sleeping bags, and backpacks. In addition, we piled on camera equipment, including tripods and both digital and film cameras, and as much Fuji Velvia slide film as we could fit in the cooler. For food, we had a stash of college road-trip staples: jerky, Swedish Fish, and granola bars, as well as lots of bottled water. It appeared that we would need to do some restocking in Mexico.

We got our first real taste of wildflowers just south of Arizona Highway 86, about an hour west of

Tucson. Brilliant yellow Gordon's bladderpod (*Lesquerella gordonii*) carpeted the hills and swathes of Mexican gold poppy trailed down distant mountains. I love Mexican gold poppy and had planted it in all of my cactus pots at home. It is one of the few wildflowers that grows well on the same watering regime as my succulent plants. Another thing I love about poppies in the *Eschscholtzia* genus is how their seedpods explode. After they have bloomed and just when the tiny corn-husk-looking pod turns tawny, the casing splits apart like it was spring-loaded, scattering seed everywhere. When I'm collecting seed, it seems like the pods will explode if I just look at them sideways. I now put a plastic bag over the entire seedpod before removing it from the plant, to avoid sending poppy seed to the four corners of my yard.

We parked the Accord by the side of the highway, slid under a barbed-wire fence, and followed our eyes into meadows of yellow and gold under the midday sun. Up to our ankles in gold, we crawled up rocky hillsides to find the best photos.

A bit later we stopped in Why, Arizona, for gas and some lunch before turning south into Organ Pipe Cactus National Monument and then into Sonora. We answered the question "Why?" with two red-chile burros (a southern Arizona term for "very large burrito"; in most of the Spanish-speaking world, a burro is simply a donkey) from the Chevron station, which I recommend as they are made by Tohono O'odham Indians who live near the station, or so the station attendants claim. I've enjoyed one of these red-chile burros on nearly every excursion I've made into Mexico via Why. The burros, which are wrapped in flour tortillas rolled so thin and with such a high lard content that they are nearly transparent, are filled with blood-red chile colorado and chunks of beef that I like to think originated in one of the skinny reservation bulls you see standing in the creosote along Highway 86. The taste can only be described as a perfect balance of red chile and fat flavor, complemented by the elasticity of the tortilla—not good for you, but very good!

Happily eating our burritos wrapped in foil, we drove out of Why and into Organ Pipe. I'm not sure if it was the shockingly pink globemallow (*Spharalcea ambigua*) or the hillsides of Mexican gold poppy, but somewhere in the middle of Organ Pipe, Simmons had a monumental burrito blowout. A huge dollop of bright red chile colorado fell out the bottom of Simmons's burrito onto the belly of his white T-shirt. The resulting stain closely resembled a shotgun blast to the stomach, making Simmons a marked man as we entered Mexico.

At Lukeville, we crossed the *frontera* (border) uneventfully and, like magic, we were in another country and another town, Lukeville's Mexican-side counterpart, Sonoyta. This was Simmons's first trip into Mexico beyond Tijuana. The state department had issued a travel warning for Americans traveling to Mexico. Apparently, Mexican President Vicente Fox's efforts to lock up some of his country's most notorious drug traffickers resulted in turf wars. The officials in Sonora said that the danger lay mostly to the east in the state of Chihuahua, along the Texas border. We hoped so. My Mexican travels had often been delayed by red tape, identity documentation, and an occasional $20 *mordida* (bribe) to traffic cops, but never by violence.

The sleepy little pueblo of Sonoyta didn't seem gripped by fear this afternoon. When we stopped at a *cervecería* (beer shop) to buy a six-pack of Dos Equis, Simmons's red-chile-stained T-shirt was about the scariest thing this town had seen in awhile. Two tall white guys, one of whom appeared to have been gut-shot, caused the cool cowboy-hat-wearing crowd under the store's awning to peer up in curiosity at Simmons's "wound." They must have believed that he was either one very

tough or very sloppy *hombre*. Our beer was packed in a plastic bag of ice, which is part of the charm of buying beer in Mexico, and as we exited the beer store, all eyes were on Simmons.

As if we hadn't made enough of a spectacle in Sonoyta, we stopped one last time before hitting the road south. Needing limes for our beer, we parked in front of a little *tienda* (store). As he walked along a display case lined with candy, the sleeve of Simmons's dreaded T-shirt caught the

Blue dicks growing along roadsides in Organ Pipe National Monument.

corner of a Tic Tac candy display, sending the little plastic dispensers all over the tile floor and providing much amusement to the sales girl, provoking giggling and ducking down behind the counter for bouts of heartier laughter. Evidently, the sight of us on our hands and knees picking up Tic Tacs was too much. As we got back into the car, I told Simmons, "Welcome to Mexico."

Since the tienda didn't have limes, we bought a rather large bag of oranges out the back of a pickup on our way out of town. Simmons, in what became his signature south-of-the-border style, stopped the Honda right in the middle of the highway to make the transaction, provoking a cacophony of horns and colorful phrases from the drivers backed up behind us.

Headed south on Highway 8, one of the best roads in northern Mexico, I explained some of the subtleties of Mexican driving to Simmons, including the not-so-subtle *tope* (TOE-pay), or speed-hump, which has a reputation for causing great undercarriage damage for unsuspecting drivers. The tope is usually, but not always, indicated by a sign with two black bumps. The tope itself can be a line of steel hemispheres bolted to the roadway or an actual asphalt hump steep enough to tear the bumper off a speeding car. Luckily, Highway 8 has no topes outside Sonoyta, and the undercarriage of Simmons's Accord was preserved for the time being.

At Sonoyta, we had two options for entering the Reserva de la Biósfera El Pinacate y Gran Desierto de Altar (the Spanish name for the Pinacate preserve area, which roughly translates into the "Pinacate and Grand Desert of Altar Biosphere Preserve"): take Highway 2 west and drop into the park from the north through some deep washes and bad roads, or continue on Highway 8, turning in at the information center on the east side of the park. A ranger at Organ Pipe Cactus National Monument, who had just returned from a trip to Pinacate, told us that we were sure to see wildflower displays on the Highway 2 route—and almost as sure to get stuck. Simmons, mustering as much bravado as someone wearing a T-shirt defiled by red chile can, exclaimed, "Don't underestimate the trusty Accord." It wasn't the reliability of Simmons's high-mileage car that worried me, but rather the car's low-clearance profile. "Look, Simmons," I said, "we have this thing loaded down like a pack mule. A kangaroo rat would barely fit between your oil pan and the road."

We decided on the easier road, Highway 8, which would take us directly into the main entrance to the park. A few kilometers south of Sonoyta, we began seeing the desert in earnest. I had Simmons slow down the Accord several times to get a closer look at big silver desert lavender (*Hyptis emoryi*) growing beside the road. In full true-blue bloom, the desert lavender got my heart racing about the wildflower possibilities to come. From childhood, all I remembered about this road were the scattered volcanic rocks, a brutal plain connecting Arizona with Rocky Point. On this trip, the view out the window framed a vibrant desert—a most excellent garden. In 1907, the first scientific expedition to the Pinacate, which was recorded in William T. Hornaday's highly colorful book, *Camp-fires on Desert and Lava*, described the area as "genuine terra incognita. While it is true that the Pinacate was known to a few Papago [now called Tohono O'odham] Indians and perhaps half a dozen Mexicans, to the reading and thinking world, it was totally unknown; the more we gathered maps and inquired about it, the less we knew." The Pinacate is so remote and untouched by humans that when the late field archaeologist and noted desert rat Julian Hayden began studying the area in 1958, he remarked that "warblers flew up to me and touched my face, a badger trotted up to me and sniffed my boot."

The entrance to the Reserva de La Biósfera de El Pinacate y Gran Desierto de Altar was dotted by a couple of neatly kept trailers, and as we approached, two attractive female park rangers riding on ATVs pulled into the parking lot. When we entered one of the trailers, a stout uniformed woman thrust clipboards at us. Where did the cute *muchachas* (girls) we had seen outside go? Attached to the clipboard was a questionnaire about our stay in the park, which with my rudimentary Spanish I translated for Simmons. When asked why we were visiting the park, I wrote in Spanish "to take photos." This, as Simmons is fond of pointing out, was our first mistake. That response prompted a series of rapid-fire follow-up questions from the officious woman, to which I mostly responded, "*Otra vez más despacio, por favor?*" (could you please repeat yourself a little slower).

Finally, a young photographer from Mexico City interceded on our behalf. He had been in the park for several weeks, photographing the desert. He began translating the bureaucratic señora's demands. It turned out that since I had disclosed that I was an author and semiprofessional photographer in the "profession" blank on the questionnaire, that Simmons was therefore my assistant and that we both would need special permission to take pictures in the park (permission that could only be granted by the director of the park, who, as luck would have it, was on a trip to Baja and

wouldn't be back until later in the evening). The photographer, Frederico, also let us know that it was customary to bring a gift to the park director when requesting permission to photograph El Pinacate. Eventually, we were granted permission to enter the park and take photos, providing we did not sell them to the Coca-Cola corporation (evidently the Mexican government had had trouble with soft-drink giants borrowing photographic renderings of their scenery without permission) and agreed to return to the office later in the evening to speak with the director.

Frederico, who by now had an interest in our project, also advised us that we would need *quatro por quatro* (four-wheel drive) to navigate many of the park's roads, and on his advice, we decided that Crater Elegante, a giant volcanic crater, would be a great destination for the afternoon. As we walked back to the car, Simmons remarked, "There are times, and this is one of them, when we shouldn't give ourselves as much credit as is due." Once back in the car, we made a pact that from then on, no matter what the circumstances, we would always be amateurs.

With the hassles of park entry behind us, we rolled down the windows and rolled down a sandy dirt road and into the heart of the Gran Desierto. Brittlebush perked up between the black rocks, and I saw the vestiges of "nama" or purple mat (*Nama hispidum*)—a little mat-forming purple flower—in the black volcanic soil. I didn't say much to Simmons, because certainly the scene was beautiful, but I was painfully aware that this wild garden had been much *more* beautiful a couple of weeks before. We had missed the apex of the bloom, but I was still certain that there were fine flowers to be found.

Simmons carefully eased the Accord up the final rocky escarpment to the trailhead of Crater Elegante. From the trailhead, the crater is not visible; only after scaling a short slope can you appreciate its grandeur. The trail we were on, which rings the rim of the crater, was an ancient game trail used by Indians hunting bighorn sheep; given that the quarry we were after was not nearly as nimble as a bighorn, our hunt would be easier, but this rim trail proved equally valuable for flower stalking. The depression is visually massive, the result of rising magma meeting groundwater and creating a steaming explosion with a force equal to an atomic blast. The largest crater in the

....
Barestem larkspur (Delphinium scaposum) *persists in the rocks of Organ Pipe National Monument.*

Pinacate, Elegante is 800 feet deep and 4,800 feet in diameter. Besides the jaw-dropping scale of the feature, the next thing that hit us was the wind. The crater seemed to create its own wind, and we were continually buffeted as we circumnavigated the rim of the crater. The ocotillos (*Fouquieria splendens*) were in peak form, and their red tips glowed as the light turned golden. Hawks and vultures rode thermals overhead, and at the bottom of the crater, a bright orange dot indicated that the entire floor was covered with Mexican gold poppies. Sometime between 5,000 and 9,000 years ago, Elegante—and the space occupied by these poppies—would have been covered with the waters of Lago ("lake") Elegante, a body of water that used to be contained within the crater. In 1907, Hornaday's outfit reacted to the Pinacate's craters like we did; he observed, "we were admiring the crater at a rate of twenty interjections a minute and the camera men were working their hardest." Clinging to the rock on the edge of the crater, we came across an aromatic elephant tree (*Bursera microphylla*), which, like the palo verde tree, is able to photosynthesize through its trunk. The little tree, twisted and picturesque in the extreme, looked like it had been carefully pruned for centuries by Japanese bonsai masters.

After stopping on the crater's rim to photograph ocotillos and a blister-beetle mating orgy, we backtracked the thirty-odd miles of dirt road to the park entrance at twilight. Along the way we snapped pictures of senita cactus (*Lophocereus schottii*) and ironwood trees (*Olneya tesota*) and even the uncommon Ajo lily (*Hesperocallis undulata*). My friend in the seed business, Rita Jo Anthony, told me that on a wet year she had taken a snapshot of her 6'3" husband standing next to an

Ajo lily that equaled his height! These lilies, while closer to two feet high, shot up a single white flower spike, straight as a surveyor's stake, into the desert air. The multiple gray ironwood trunks were intertwined in a ganglion of hairy senita arms, like two happy drunks tied together to keep upright. I thought, here is a stellar example of combining plants with different textures in desert gardens— succulents and evergreen legume trees with lilies beneath—combinations with drama that are easy to replicate in more domesticated settings. I remembered that at the Arizona–Sonora Desert Museum one of my favorite gardens has as its centerpiece a large ironwood whose branches crawl with a climbing cactus. As I took pictures, I thought, "Ah ha! Here is my new media-savvy design concept—snakes in trees."

Characteristic of deserts, the late afternoon light was clear and warm and perfect for making photos. There was a stillness and clarity in the warm air that felt palpable. Back at park head-quarters, we were greeted by one of the cute ATV-riding rangers, who informed us that the park director had not yet returned. At this juncture, we were not completely dismayed by the park director's absence. We had prepared to surrender our Dos Equis as a gift, but we wondered what else in our dwindling larder we might need to fork over to preserve our good standing in the park.

By this time, we had worked up a hunger that could not be satiated by Swedish Fish and granola bars. Faced with a long drive back down a dirt road in the dark, a dinner of junk food provisions, and setting up camp in the dark, we made a bold decision: we would drive south on Highway 8 to the touristy beach town of Puerto Peñasco (aka Rocky Point) and enjoy sea-ray tacos and Negro Modelo beer at Flavio's by the ocean. Once in Rocky Point, we could find a cheap motel to crash at, get up at 4:00 a.m., and drive to the northern end of the park to catch the wildflowers in the first light of day. Frederico had mentioned that the dunes on the northern side of the park would have more flowers in peak bloom than we would see around the craters.

At Flavio's, we looked at the lights on Cholla Bay and downed tacos, salsa, and beer until we could eat no more. We found a reasonable little motel on the outskirts of town and hit the sack, dreaming of black rocks and ocotillo.

Aside from barking dogs, noisy semis, and an annoying cricket that troubled Simmons, we slept great. We awoke to early-morning fog and zipped up Highway 8 in the dark. After making it back to Sonoyta, we turned west onto Highway 2 and began paying attention to kilometer markers. We had learned from Frederico that kilometer markers 72 and 79 were the best places along Highway 2 to find wildflowers. Our immediate destination, a place known as Microondas ("microwaves"), was a small volcanic hill dotted with radio towers and surrounded by dunes. Simmons eased the Accord off the highway onto a cobblestone road. Even in darkness, it was obvious that we were surrounded by flowers. The air was fecund and wet with a green vegetative dampness. Right away, I spotted bird-cage primrose (*Oenothera deltoides*, also called dune evening primrose), bright white, beside the road. The air was crisp, and it felt good to emerge from the Honda and stretch our legs. Eagerly, I began setting up my tripod, grabbing film from the cooler, and rushing into the dunes. The golden dunes, the

Ajo lily—one of the floral wonders of a wet year in the Pinacate.

black mountains to the north, the pale blue sky—this was going to be a banner morning. Sure enough, the sun rose and the light that we had arisen so early to catch began to reveal itself. Choked with desert sunflower (*Geraea canescens*), dune evening primrose (*Oenothera deltoides*), and sand verbena (*Abronia villosa*), the dunes were filled with surprises. Here and there, a blue palo verde (*Parkinsonia florida*) rose from the sand. Like lizards we skittered up and down the dunes, our big eyes peering through viewfinders, snapping off photos. Speaking of reptiles, these very dunes are home to the fringe-toed lizard, whose fan-like rear feet are made for dune running, and western shovelnose snakes, who can slither *under* the sand to hide. The conditions couldn't have been better; there was no wind, the flowers were fully open, and the light was luminous but not yet severe. Racing the rising sun, we burned through film and megabytes as fast as we could, hoping for one or two real standouts that would hint at the grandeur of this ephemeral event on these remote dunes. At one moment during the morning, I found myself in a sandy hollow beneath a blue palo verde tree—my only company a curve-billed thrasher. I looked behind me at Simmons, about a half-mile away, wet to the hips from bushwhacking through dense dew-covered flowers, camera in hand. Seeing Simmons in all of these flowers on the ocean-like dunes brought a line from one of Simmons's poems to mind:

> Finally it is spring—
> it seems as if even these vast seas
> know the changes. They are richer ...

As the light changed from a luminous morning glow to blindingly bright, we packed up the car and toasted the wildflowers of the Microondas with two of the beers earmarked for the park director. Ravenous, we followed the beers with a few Sonoyta oranges, and the combination tasted surprisingly good. Although it was only 9:00 a.m. when we rolled into Sonoyta, we found an open taco stand for one last meal in Mexico. By afternoon we'd be back in Tucson, by Thursday morning we'd be back at work. But this morning, like a glowing yellow sunflower, a French-curve-shaped dune, or a jagged line of black mountains, was burned into our memories. Through our spontaneous twenty-eight-hour indulgence, we had claimed a little piece of the fabulous spring bloom of 2005.

Plants to find

Ajo lily (*Hesperocallis undulata*)

arroyo lupine (*Lupinus sparsiflorus*)

barestem larkspur (*Delphinium scaposum*)

blue dicks (*Dichelostemma pulchellum*)

blue palo verde (*Parkinsonia florida,* formerly *Cercidium floridum*)

brittlebush (*Encelia farinosa*)

desert lavender (*Hyptis emoryi*)

desert peppergrass (*Ledidium fremontii*)

desert sunflower (*Geraea canescens*)

dune evening primrose (*Oenothera deltoides*)

elephant tree (*Bursera microphylla*)

globemallow (*Spharalcea ambigua*)

Gordon's bladderpod (*Lesquerella gordonii*)

ironwood tree (*Olneya tesota*)

Mexican gold poppy (*Eschscholtzia mexicana*)

ocotillo (*Fouquieria splendens*)

purple mat, nama (*Nama hispidum*)

sand verbena (*Abronia villosa*)

senita cactus (*Lophocereus schottii*)

Pinacate Biosphere Reserve

Pinacate's information center is located just off Highway 8, at kilometer post 52, 32 miles south of Lukeville, Arizona. You can contact the reserve as follows:

Reserva de la Biósfera El Pinacate y Gran
    Desierto de Altar
Apartado Postal #125
Puerto Peñasco, Sonora, Mexico 83550
phone 011-62-159864
fax 011-62-146508

Where to camp

El Tecolote ("the owl")
In the Pinacate reserve (register at Pinacate's information center)
Capacity: 40 people
Location: 5 miles northeast of Crater Elegante
Best for visitors to the volcanic craters and hiking trails.

Cono Rojo ("red cone")
In the Pinacate reserve (register at Pinacate's information center)
Capacity: 20 people
Location: 14 miles northwest of the info center

Backcountry camping
Limited to 3 per party; campsite must be located at least 1/2 mile from any road or crater.

Where to stay in Rocky Point

Viña del Mar Hotel
The chief virtue of the Viña del Mar hotel is its proximity to Flavio's (see "Where to Eat") and the Old Port (El Puerto).

Calle Primero de Junio y Malecón Kino S/N Col. El Puerto
Puerto Peñasco, Sonora, Mexico 83550
Phone (01-638) 383-3600 or (01-638) 383-0100
www.vinadelmarhotel.com

Where to eat

Flavio's, or as their sign proclaims, **"Aquí es con Flavio."**
Located at the end of the Malecón in the Old Port near the fish market. For open-air dining, quick service, good beer, ceviche, and tacos, Flavio's is hard to beat. Almost worth the drive in from the Pinacate just for the food.

What to read

Camp-Fires on Desert and Lava, by William T. Hornaday. Published in 1908, re-issued by University of Arizona Press, 1983 (now out of print).

Riverfall, by Simmons B. Buntin. Salmon Publishing, 2005.

The Sierra Pinacate, by Julian D. Hayden; with photographs by Jack Dykinga and essays by Charles Bowden and Bernard L. Fontana. University of Arizona Press, 1998.

Sonora: An Intimate Geography, by David Yetman. University of New Mexico Press, 2000.

Sonoran Desert Plants: An Ecological Atlas, by Raymond Turner, Janice Emily Bowers, and Tony L. Burgess. University of Arizona Press, 1995.

Sonoran Desert Wildflowers: A Field Guide to the Common Wildflowers of the Sonoran Desert, by Richard Spellenberg. Falcon, 2002.

A Westerly Trend, by Godfrey Sykes. University of Arizona Press, 1945.

Wildflowers of the Desert Southwest, by Meg Quinn. Rio Nuevo Publishers, 2000.

Be Your Own Shaman: Sedona

When: *late April 2005*

Destination: *Arizona Highway 179 south of Sedona*

Total trip time: *28 hours*

Vehicle: *1999 VW Jetta TDI*

Roundtrip distance from Tucson: *592 miles*

Traveling companion: *just the iPod*

Music: *Iron and Wine's* Our Endless Numbered Days; *Hem's* Eveningland

ON MY WAY TO A BOOK SIGNING in Sedona, I spent the night with my parents in Mesa, and after catching up with Mom and Dad the next morning I headed north on I-17. The shoulders of the roads around suburban Phoenix were still thick with growth from the unusually heavy winter rains of 2005, but the late spring heat was turning most of what had been chromium-yellow desert marigolds (*Baileya multiradiata*) and orange globemallow plants into straw-colored brush.

As the road climbed up Black Canyon out of Phoenix, I began to informally caravan with a convertible Bentley. The whole car was a paradox

The sweetly scented Palmer's penstemon welcomes travelers to Sedona along Highway 179.

of sorts. It had the New York vanity plate "ABUELITA" (little grandma), with a Scottsdale Rolls Royce license plate surround. The woman at the wheel, a stylish brunette in sunglasses who looked to me not at all like a little grandma, wore a lime-green blouse with a pink scarf blowing in the wind. In the front seat next to her was a younger brunette, probably in her twenties, and in the backseat an even younger teenaged girl—daughters? Granddaughters?

We took turns passing each other on the climb up to Cordes Junction and winding down through the Verde Valley. I was listening to the New York-based band Hem, which sounds more like a band from Appalachia or rural Georgia, but it was good music and the first line from an old Johnny Cash song called "Jackson": "We got married in a fever, hotter than a pepper sprout," got me thinking about my own short engagement.

When we got married, August 21, 1989, we were both twenty-two years old. My wife, Deirdre, who has the milky, freckled skin of a strawberry blonde, didn't look a day over sixteen. Our courtship consisted of driving all over southern Utah in my convertible Fiat Spyder. Since we are both oldest children, who both think we know best, our relationship has rarely been smooth. A week before our wedding, I tried to drive all night from Provo, Utah, to Mesa, Arizona. Just outside of Parowan, Utah, I fell asleep at the wheel, rear-ended a van, knocked out one of my front teeth, and totaled my Fiat. A few young men would have taken this as a sign or at least a warning—I didn't.

Deirdre, whose hair is truly more strawberry than blonde, exhibits many of the stereotypical characteristics of redheads: she is fiery-tempered, stubborn, and resistant to authority, especially mine. After reading an article about redheads and commenting that I now understood her resistance to my authority, she smiled and replied, "What authority?"

At the Sedona exit off I-17, I was surprised to see that my fellow travelers in the Bentley continued north. I had pegged them as Sedona-bound, fully expecting to see them pull into the Sedona Radisson or some other appropriately posh accommodation. But just like that, this affluent family whooshed up I-17 with their hair and scarves blowing in the wind.

Once onto Highway 179, red rocks in the distance, I rolled down the windows and began to take in the scenery in earnest. For some reason, I

hadn't expected to see much in the way of wildflowers on this trip and I had left my Fuji Velvia film in the refrigerator and my Nikon camera in the closet. The only camera in my possession was my little Canon G2 digital, which I usually use as a backup. A few miles down Highway 179, I realized that leaving my best camera at home might have been a serious mistake. Out of the red soil, I began to see thick polka-dot patterns of white flowers. Unprepared for botanical splendor, I couldn't immediately identify these vigorous bloomers. I'd been driving around like a dope, thinking about my marriage and my life and ignoring prime wildflowers at their peak. Idiot! Refocusing my energies, I got back into the moment. Could these little white jewels be blackfoot daisies (*Melampodium leucanthum*)? I had

Who can resist blackfoot daisies and red rocks?

Palmer's penstemon bloom stalks can reach heights of 6 feet.

Mixed in with these flowers was a low-growing banana yucca (*Yucca baccata*), whose sickle-shaped blossoms resemble its namesake. I thought to myself: Here I have it, the perfect wild-plant combination for much of high-elevation Arizona—Palmer's penstemon, Engelmann's hedgehog cactus (*Echinocereus engelmannii*), blackfoot daisy, and banana yucca. What else could you need to make a heart-stopping red-rock garden? Red rocks, I suppose.

I ducked between the strands of a barbed-wire fence and hiked up an escarpment to a large red-rock slope with loads of blackfoot daisy once again dotting the rocks. The wet winter of 2005 had kept on giving. I reluctantly got back in the car to make it to my signing on time, but I would be back this way in the afternoon—this I knew.

I spent the afternoon outside the Storyteller bookstore at Tlaquepaque Village, a quaint shopping plaza by the banks of Oak Creek. Tlaquepaque is a rather convincing faux Mexican village filled with jewelry stores, galleries, and a good representation of the ubiquitous new god of the Southwest: Kokopelli. Situated outside in one of the little alleys of the cobblestone village, I had a small table stacked with copies of my first book, *Yard Full of Sun: The Story of a Gardener's Obsession That Got a Little Out of Hand*. Book signings can shake an author's confidence. Although the book was garnering lavish reviews and would later win a 2006 American Horticultural Society Book Award, on that Saturday at Tlaquepaque, no one was buying, and in fact, there were just not many people passing by. I watched a happy young bride and groom exiting the plaza's wedding chapel, made small-talk with passing shoppers, and listened to the wind rustle the sycamore leaves.

tried growing them and, more often than not, failed on account of poor drainage, yet here they were, thriving on red-hot hardscrabble slopes in ineffable abundance. Just as I was trying to cope with the beauty of the daisies against the red dirt, I turned a corner and found colonies of the pinkest Palmer's penstemon (*Penstemon palmeri*) I'd ever seen, up against the rock cutaway of a curve in the road. Nearly tearing the oil pan off my car (something I've done before when searching for flowers), I pulled off the highway in a less-than-ideal spot.

People are understandably leery of kiosk-style vendors at shopping malls, and even in this upscale village that could hardly be considered a mall, some looked at me as if I was a young huckster trying to sell them a new cell-phone calling plan. "No, really," I wanted to say. "It's a fun book, you'll enjoy it, it might enrich your life." I was in need of Kokopelli's flute playing, or some other Sedona-appropriate gimmick, to lure in potential customers. In the book-signing game, I always carry a spare case of books in my trunk in case the store runs low, and when I have to break into that box, I know I've done well. On the flip side, you know the turnout was off when the bookstore sends out their accountant to buy a book from you, especially when that is the only copy you sell. Ouch! It was a good thing that I knew that wildflowers were just down the road. I hoped they could redeem the trip.

I blasted out of Tlaquepaque in a jangle of Kokopelli wind chimes, ready to return to the always-generous flora. I stopped at the mile marker where I had noticed the blackfoot daisies on my way into town. I slid back through the barbed wire again and up to a little slope of red sandstone, polka-dotted with blackfoot daisy. With no tripod and a little camera, I rolled around on the sandstone, angling for the best photos, making the best human tripod I could. I wandered back around through a big clump of banana yucca, shooting photos as big clouds drifted overhead. I ambled down around the roadside until I found a big rocky cliff next to the road-cut, filled with iridescent pink Palmer's

penstemon, one of the few scented members of this large genus (also called scented penstemon for that reason). As evening came, the sweet waxy aroma of penstemon wafted around me as I snapped photos while traffic buzzed by.

I wondered why more of these luxury cars and RVs weren't stopping. As far as I was concerned, these flowers were more interesting than any chrome cowboy sculptures in Sedona. Really, this landscape was more colorful and resonant than most of the art I had spied at the roadside galleries. And wildflowers are an egalitarian art form and can be enjoyed by anyone. Where was my New York *abuelita*? If she was not already wrapped in towels with cucumbers over her eyes, I had the feeling she might enjoy this. Perhaps this was why I was alone in this rocky floral wonderland—too much ensconcing in luxury and New Age shaman teachings led to landscape blindness.

I, for one, felt that I had found my own "vortex," based on the divine vegetation. I lay down on red sand on the blackfoot-daisy slope and watched the big clouds moving until the light was almost gone. I was prostrate below the cosmos—ready for a winged spirit woman, a unicorn, a wise toad, or a talking coyote to advise a middle-aged guy who was becoming good at breaking all the rules of how to be an adult. I lay on my back spread-eagled for some time, waiting for some midlife-crisis guidance counseling, just a thirty-nine-year-old father with a thirteen-year-old daughter and a wife who knew all his tricks. I had taken the on-ramp to the wildflower highway, and I was bound to learn something—maybe even something about myself. Before any more inspiration came, a red ant went up the leg of my pants and I jumped up to kill it before it headed too far me, I could summon my own spring blackfoot-daisy-and-penstemon vortex, hanging in the air, complete with scent, color, and red rocks. It was enough to align every chakra in my wildflower soul.

Plants to find

banana yucca *(Yucca baccata)*
blackfoot daisy *(Melampodium leucanthum)*
desert marigold *(Baileya multiradiata)*
Engelmann's hedgehog cactus *(Echinocereus engelmannii)*
Palmer's penstemon, scented penstemon, wild pink snapdragon, giant snapdragon *(Penstemon palmeri)*

Where to eat

Pizza Picazzo
There are not many places to eat in Sedona that aren't overpriced for so-so food. Most pies here are under 20 bucks. Try the artichoke-chicken pizza.
1855 West Highway 89A
Sedona, Arizona
928-282-4140

Where to stay

Sedona Wildflower Inn
If you have money falling out of your pockets, there are lots of high-end resorts to try, but the Wildflower Inn is a good value for the rest of us.
6086 Highway 179
Sedona, Arizona
928-284-3937, www.sedonawildflowerinn.com

What to read

Arizona's Best Wildflower Hikes: The High Country, by Christine Maxa. Westcliffe Publishers, 2002.

Traditionally used for food, footwear, and shampoo, the banana yucca is as handsome as it is useful.

north. And with that, I got in the car and drove south into the night.

On the way home, I felt grateful for a half-day among wildflowers in a great and maybe sacred place. I decided that I didn't need the spirit woman, the unicorn, or the coyote. When you carry the memories of flowers inside—their scents, their delicate constructions, their sturdy stems— you become your own Sedona shaman. If I closed my eyes and focused on a spot three feet ahead of

Infidel in the Dunes: Coral Pink Sand Dunes

When: June 30, 2005
Destination: Coral Pink Sand Dunes, Utah
Vehicle: 1999 VW Jetta TDI
Roundtrip distance from Tucson: 580 miles
Traveling companions: Deirdre, my wife, and Zoë, our daughter
Music: Country music and farm report,
KONY-FM radio out of St. George, Utah

FOUR MONTHS AFTER my whirlwind trip to the Pinacate, I was still chasing wildflowers on sand dunes. The wildflower bloom season that began back in February in Mexico had moved north, climbing to higher elevations and cooler microclimates in hard-to-predict waves. The element of surprise egged me on. The possibility of blossoms in the badlands, flowers in dry arroyos at the end of some unnamed desert dirt road, made the chase irresistible.

Field guides were imprecise when it came to predicting the actual location and timing of wildflower events. For this particular trip, I e-mailed the ranger

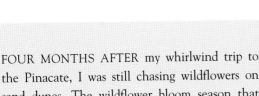
Around the Fourth of July, rough mules ears orchestrate their own fireworks in Utah's Coral Pink Sand Dunes State Park.

at Coral Pink Sand Dunes State Park, but as he informed me in his response, he had only been there for a few weeks and was still trying to "figure out what bloomed when." It is precisely the unquantifiable behavior of wildflowers that will possess a man to drive across state lines, mountain ranges, and international borders with little more than a ragged guidebook, an old map, and a wild look in his eyes.

In our Tucson garden, June is the cruelest month. All my beloved penstemons were dried up and dormant, and my bat-faced cuphea (*Cuphea llavea*) leaves, unhappy with my once-a-week watering regime, were wilted over, their leaf tips the texture of potato chips. Leaving the desert in June for higher country always feels like the great escape, and as I packed up the car in my swimming suit on an already 90-degree morning, as much as I love the heat, I couldn't help but smile at the thought of ponderosa pines and cool weather, pink dunes and yellow flowers.

By the time we set out from Tucson, the temperature was pushing 105. My wife, Deirdre, her hair still wet from the pool, was seated shotgun, and thirteen-year-old Zoë was riding hump in the back seat. Zoë's increasingly long legs were stretched out between the front seats with her toes up by the gearshift, an awkward arrangement for everyone except her. Our ride, a VW Jetta with its turbo diesel engine, was becoming too small for our family, but we were resisting the pull of the SUV. Even though we were occasionally hit with repairs requiring expensive German parts, we happily paid; the Jetta was an economy car, and on a good day we could drive from Los Angeles to Tucson on one tank of diesel. Even though having two companions filled our compact car, it was nice to have Deirdre and Zoë traveling with me, seeing that Deirdre was usually teaching, and Zoë was often busy with volleyball and ballet practices. For them, the magic of wildflower hunts had worn thin, and Zoë was often unable to suppress a groan as I pulled the car onto the shoulder to observe some special plant. However, they were both keen on the idea of Utah milkshakes, the prospect of which I held out like an Oreo of encouragement. I agreed to let them sleep in on my early-morning ventures.

Two months before our trip, I had left my full-time job as a nursery manager to write about and design gardens. This trip to Utah was my inaugural voyage of sorts as a self-employed father, and the feeling of freedom was delicious. I thought to myself, "I'm on a trip, with the sole purpose of writing about and taking pictures of flowers, and I'm doing it with my family, at my own pace." Even driving our old Jetta, I felt richer than a Hollywood divorce lawyer.

Our first hint of wildflower excitement began in the late afternoon, fifty miles north of Flagstaff on Highway 89, on the Navajo Nation. Beneath orange mesas and sandstone fins, with snow-capped mountains in the background, I spied what at first appeared to be bunches of phlox beside the road. Much to Zoë's chagrin, I insisted on pulling over for a closer look. The sun, partly veiled by the smoke from wildfires in Utah, gave the desert sky a strange hazy look, in contrast to its usual clear azure. I only mention the light because, as any photographer who has spent time taking pictures in the desert will tell you, the full midday light on a sunny day usually makes for brutally overexposed pictures. Armed with my old Nikon and a cold new roll of film from the ice chest, I ran across the road, avoiding reservation dogs and "cruise America" RVs. I knelt down by the side of the road to take pictures of a flower that I now recognized was not phlox at all, but rather a plant from my favorite genus—a penstemon, and more specifically, a sand penstemon (*Penstemon ambiguous*).

This plant, in a family known for tall architectural spires, is an exception. Its other common name, bush penstemon, is more apt. The low-growing little plant really looks like a small shrub

The aptly named Penstemon ambiguous *glows beside Highway 89 on the Navajo Reservation north of Flagstaff.*

with the top of its head coiffured with pink flowers. One of the pleasures of taking photos of flowers is that, as with gardening, you have to get down on the level of the plants. As a tall person (I'm 6'3"), I've always considered it a great irony that my life's work involves stooping down to observe, photograph, plant, and groom wild and domesticated flora. I've never cared a whit for looking up and identifying stars or planets, preferring to enjoy them in a more general way, as in "look at all the stars up there." As I've said, often unpopularly in a town full of astronomers and stargazers: Some people like looking up and some down; I prefer looking down.

This was my first time seeing sand penstemon growing in the wild, and it was love at first sight. I never forget the first time I see a particular species of flower in the wild. Growing out of the red cinders by the roadside on a hot June afternoon, the sand penstemon looked otherworldly—an impression I often have about desert flowers that are thriving in some ungodly nook by, or out of, rock or gravel, or beside a flaming expanse of asphalt highway.

In the past, our stops on the Navajo Nation have been short and of the commercial variety. Perhaps we are as charmed as New Yorkers moving to Santa Fe and decorating entire homes with kokopelli statuettes, but we've always loved Native American arts and crafts. On our honeymoon, we stopped at a roadside kiosk near Cameron, where Deirdre bought me a silver Zuni ring that has, from time to time (because I dislike wearing any jewelry, even watches), served as my wedding band. We have also purchased beaded necklaces, turquoise rings, and wool Navajo rugs. I've even admired the clever and kitschy billboards for the Chief Yellowhorse Trading Post announcing "friendly Indians ahead" and later, when you've driven past, "friendly Indians behind you."

This appreciation of things Native American has extended to geology, and certainly no one can dispute that the Navajo Nation is full of excellent rock formations that never fail to inspire awe. Curiously, the Navajo Nation, at least along Highway 89, has resisted the temptation to sparkle up the roadside with a series of glittering casinos and houses of wagering tucked indiscreetly into gas stations. For the time being, the trip from Flagstaff to Page is still punctuated by herds of goats, octagonal homes, and stone trading posts with a few gas stations—in a word, unspoiled.

I hunkered down to photograph the penstemon and looked around for landmarks. To my sensibilities, citing a prominent mesa or sandstone spire in the background of a wildflower photo gives a much-desired effect. Giving geology a place in desert gardens is sometimes hard to do. A landscape-architect friend from Albuquerque, David Cristiani, thinks that designers who have not embraced a desert aesthetic try to "hide the ground" with too many plants. The spaces between plants and the rocks between plants are *worth* something. Another friend of mine—this one in the seed business, Rita Jo Anthony—says that she appreciates the desert because "you can see each plant as opposed to just a forest of plants." I thought about the Navajos living out under those tabletop mesas, raising sheep, weaving blankets, or perhaps surfing the Internet. Still, I couldn't help humming the John Prine song, "and tourist, in the badlands, taking pictures of the Navajo, every time he clicks, his Kodak pics, he steals a little bit of soul, uh-oh."

This road, Highway 89, was a well-known route to me. How many times had I been down this highway? Traveling with my parents as a young boy to visit grandparents north of Salt Lake City; driving my first car, the old Fiat Spyder convertible, to college at Brigham Young University and later to the University of Utah; on my honeymoon with my wife, Deirdre, driving a Pontiac Firebird with "just married" spelled out with Oreo cookies on the back window; driving my daughter and niece back to Arizona in a VW camper van.

All trips considered, back and forth to school for Christmas and summer breaks, moving from Arizona to Utah and back to Arizona again in a twenty-four-foot-long Ryder truck, I must have driven Highway 89 forty times.

More so than anywhere else in the U.S., entering southern Utah is like crossing the border into a foreign country. Say hello to grasshopper milkshakes (Oreo cookies and chocolate-mint ice cream) you eat with a spoon, and very polite young waitresses of northern European descent. The predominant religion, Mormonism, influences everything from the politics to the architecture to popular culture in Utah, and even to a nonbeliever like myself it is both a comfort and a disturbance. For someone who lived in Utah and is returning to visit, the general tidiness of the streets and gardens, the lack of minorities, and yes, even the prevalence of apple beer is remarkable. In many ways, the values of Mormonism are my values: the importance of thrift, family, education, hard work, and strong ethics are hard to argue against. I should disclose that I was raised a Mormon, yet I have not practiced my religion for almost twenty years. I have become a nonbeliever, an outsider, or to use the popular term in the interior West, a "Jack Mormon."

Regardless of my standing in the Mormon Church, I can't help but be impressed with the layout and endurance of the Mormon village. Yes, there is the same prejudice and closed-mindedness that you find in most small towns, but there is also a friendliness and worldly dialog that makes a Mormon town different. Because of the Church's evangelical efforts, many of the men and some of the women in any given town have traveled abroad and are fluent in a foreign language. When entering Utah from Arizona on Highway 89, Kanab is the first real Mormon town in a long string stretching from here clear up past Salt Lake City and into Idaho. In many ways, Kanab is the gateway into another world.

Ever since my siblings and I were kids, an overnight stay at Parry Lodge in Kanab has been a treat. Once housing the likes of John Wayne, Gabby Hayes, and other Western stars, the lodge hasn't changed much since the 1950s, which was fine with Deirdre, Zöe, and me. In the evening, we walked around town while leather-clad German tourists sputtered and popped up and down the main drag on rented Harleys. We had dinner at a diner with biscuits and gravy, and then listened to a bluegrass band in a band shell next to the Mormon church. Kanab is a town in hot pursuit of a new identity. Gourmet coffee shops and even vegetarian restaurants have appeared among the usual shake and English-chip stands. If not for the prominent church building, the main drag in Kanab could almost be mistaken for that of a hip Colorado mining-turned-tourist town. Almost. Thankfully, you only need to walk one block off the commercial strip to find all the underpinnings of a Mormon village firmly in place. The wide tree-lined streets, the large old homes in a state of benign disrepair, look the same as ever.

After dinner, we took a family swim back at Parry Lodge in the same kidney-shaped pool that I swam in as a kid. Like me, Zoë loves to swim, and we got our money's worth at the lodge, alternating between the heated spa (or as Zoë calls it, "the jacooz") and the much cooler swimming pool. Out swimming with Zoë, it was a little terrifying to think of myself as the parent of a teenage daughter. I had always hoped that my daughter would be bookish, introspective, interested in plants, and perhaps play the clarinet in the band. Zoë was a smart girl who had eagerly read the entire Harry Potter series and all of Sharon Creech's titles, but I was out of luck in the plant and clarinet departments. Looking at my daughter, I realized that what I had produced was a bombshell blonde who could crack jokes and play ball and carry on a lively conversation with just about anyone. The time was coming very soon when she would get a lot of attention from boys. I thought of the Yeats poem, "A Prayer for My Daughter," in which the poet considers the dangers of gorgeousness for girls:

May she be granted beauty and yet not
Beauty to make a stranger's eye distraught,
Or hers before a looking glass, for such,
Being made beautiful overmuch,
Consider beauty a sufficient end …

Careful not to disturb my slumbering girls, I crept out of Parry Lodge at 4:00 a.m., driving west out of Kanab on Highway 89. Just a little way up the road and I would be smack-dab in the heart of Mormon country. I thought of the little towns of Mt. Carmel Junction and especially of Orderville. In his classic work of nonfiction, *Mormon Country*, Wallace Stegner described Orderville as an "Arcadian" village, which practiced a brand of Mormon communism that required the sharing of all material possessions. For eleven years from the early 1870s to the early 1880s, the little community thrived, until the surrounding mining operations began siphoning the town's young people away for better-paying jobs and more of the luxuries of American life.

In my adult life, I have done about everything I could to shake off the trappings of my Mormon past. I have been embarrassed about the church's parochial stance on a variety of social issues. When asked where I was from, I often responded "Phoenix" instead of "Mesa," to avoid a follow-up question regarding my religion. Yes, I had been raised, baptized, served a two-year Mormon mission as a nineteen-year-old kid, and been married in the Mormon temple not long after that, but I resisted being defined by it. Following our marriage, Deirdre and I embarked on an extended sabbatical from all things Mormon.

But driving into this part of southern Utah, I can't help being seduced by the pastoral villages and the awesome red-rock geology of the area. From what I can see, this is the most picturesque scenery in America. The Mormon villages are well-conceived agrarian towns with the homes neatly clustered in grids around a commercial town center. They are a fine example of how civilization (on a small scale) and wilderness can complement one another.

I passed Moqui Cave in the pitch-black night. For the first time in a long while, I felt proud of my Mormon heritage. I realized that these Mormons were outsiders and dissenters of the first order. From 1847, well into the beginning of the twentieth century, Mormons were often at odds with the U.S. government. The Mormons had come from the poorest villages of Great Britain and Scandinavia and pushed across the Rocky Mountains, burying their dead in shallow graves along the way. Going against the advice of other church members, Brigham Young refused to cross the Sierras to the more fertile fields of California, settling instead in the high valleys of the Great Basin—places he suspected no one else would want. So now, driving through Mormon country, I felt a certain kinship with my defiant ancestors. In the nineteenth century, Mormons ranked right alongside Cochise, Geronimo, and Butch Cassidy as the ultimate rebels and outsiders seeking refuge in the West. For all their historical umbrage with the U.S. government, it's a perverse twist that Mormons are now prominent conservative political figures, consummate Washington insiders, and mostly right-leaning conservatives.

I'm sorry to say I flattened a rabbit with my right front tire just after the turn into Coral Pink Sand Dunes State Park, and the jolt shook me from my thoughts of Mormonism to the task at hand: wildflower hunting. When I arrived at the visitors center, mine was the only car in the lot and the sky was just beginning to show the first stratified rays of morning. I reached into the cooler and pulled out a Starbucks double-shot cappuccino to help wake me up. Even now, I find drinking coffee in Utah more pleasurable because of the taboo against it. In that early light, what I came to photograph began to take shape. The park, only a few miles outside Kanab, is composed of some unbelievably luxurious orange-pink sand. Its grains are finer and softer than any beach sand I've ever set foot on. The only downside of Coral Pink Sand Dunes State Park is its "multiuse" mandate by the state of Utah. What multiuse translates to is "all-terrain vehicles" and other noisy dune-chewing machines. Coral Pink Sand Dunes is a small park, only 2,500 acres total, but on holiday weekends as many as 1,000 vehicles may be out on the dunes. As Janice Emily Bowers says in her book, *Dune Country*, "the contest is an uneven one: when dune meets dune buggy, the dune usually loses." Thankfully, there were no off-road vehicles allowed in the park before 9:00 a.m. on the day I was there.

As I unpacked my gear on the first dune, I realized that, once again, I had forgotten my tripod in Tucson, making photos in the early light very difficult. I resigned myself to lying down in the dunes, as I had on the red rocks near Sedona. My tripod forgetfulness was turning me into a decent human tripod, and bracing against the leeward sides of the dunes was as comfortable as sitting in a poolside lounge chair and provided a flower's-eye view. It occurred to me that this gave a whole new meaning to the term "sandbagging."

The dunes were lousy with rough mules ears (*Wyethia scabra*). The rough mules ears formed giant yellow and green hemispheres that dotted the crests and valleys of the dunes. Walking on the powder-soft dunes in the early morning was sensual, and the gentle s-curves and hollows reminded me, more than anything else, of a woman's body. The sand, blown smooth by the wind, was like skin. It was early and quiet; my footprints were the only tracks on the dunes. As the horizon began to glow with the first hint of

Young ponderosa pines await their sandy fate

was a pretty silver-blue, providing a softer lacey counterpoint to the yucca. This landscape, with its curves and undulations, stretched out before me like a reclining centerfold. It was almost too much beauty for one man to absorb. Before the sun crested the eastern ridge of the park, I had shot three rolls of film. I felt greedy and aroused, like some kind of landscape pornographer. I gripped my Starbucks can and camera bags and headed deep into the dunes—an infidel inside the

Kanab yucca standing watch at the crest of a dune.

sun, the valleys and peaks of the dunes glowed with yellow mules ear flowers. I lay prostrate on the dunes like a sniper and practiced breathing slowly, so as not to jiggle the camera in the slightest as I released the shutter. Balancing my camera on a split-rail fence (erected to keep out the dune shredders from a little area), I slowed down the shutter speed and increased my depth of field to capture a basin full of sand sage (*Artemisia filifolia*), Kanab yucca (*Yucca kanabensis*), and rough mules ears. Kanab yucca, like many in its genus, is a low rosette with bold spear-like flower spikes rising several feet above the ground. The sand sage

Zion curtain (a term coined by Salt Lake's KRCL radio—"radio behind the Zion curtain"; the "Zion curtain" surrounds the Mormon-dominated portions of the intermountain West and is not to be confused with Zion National Park). Astonished at my solitude, I hiked for a couple of hours in the cool morning to a place where ponderosa pines grew straight out of the dunes.

Coral Pink Sand Dunes State Park is the only place on the earth where sand dunes support large pine trees, although "support" may not be the right word. The ponderosa pines (*Pinus ponderosa*) are here only because the pink dunes move very slowly, only a foot or two each year, allowing the seeds to germinate and the trees to reach adolescence. Yet however slow, the march of the dunes is inexorable, and eventually the ponderosas will suffocate and die as sand piles up onto the plants' root zones. At Coral Pink, half the pines are heathy and young and half are dead.

Making my way back across the dunes, I spotted a bluish-purple flower coming directly out of the dunes. Silvery sophora (*Sophora stenophylla*), true to its name, has silvery foliage and is a cousin to a popular Arizona landscape plant, Texas mountain laurel (*Sophora secundiflora*). One of the plants prized by botanists hunting for obscurities, and a plant that I missed, was Welsh's milkweed (*Asclepias welshii*), which is endemic (grows only there) to the park.

I felt lucky that the park was not whining with quads and dune buggies and the mullet-coiffed camping crowd. Still, the vehicle tracks on some of the dunes bothered me. I found myself drawn to the part of the park that was untrammeled by gasoline-powered intruders. Of all the different types of desert terrain, sand dunes seem the most

A lone silvery sophora makes its blue presence known.

misunderstood and abused. Those who consider sand dunes wastelands have never seen them exploding with rough mules ears in late June. Dunes and their plant communities are vibrant and alive (or sleeping) and changing all the time. Being able to adapt quickly to change is key to staying alive here. One of the key adaptations of many dune plants is the ability to form adventitious roots and to grow rapidly. Adventitious roots form on the stem or trunk of a plant, and in dune country, the ability to promptly spout these new roots when a plant gets buried by sand is

paramount to the plant's survival. The Kanab yucca can form them, and the ponderosa pine cannot, and that spells slow death for the ponderosa.

The sun rose in smoky-orange forest-fire haze. I had burned through my film, finished my Starbucks, and managed to fill all my pockets with salmon-colored sand. I felt full of beauty, like one of the outrageous yellow rough mules ears I had been photographing. There was no escaping the fact that I was an infidel in Zion, but even with a double-shot cappuccino can rolling around on the floorboards, I drove back into Kanab feeling like a man redeemed by coral sand and yellow flowers named after the ears of pack animals.

. . . .

Plants to find

big sagebrush *(Artemisia tridentata)*
Kanab yucca *(Yucca kanabensis)*
ponderosa pine *(Pinus ponderosa)*
rough mules ears *(Wyethia scabra)*
sand penstemon *(Penstemon ambiguous)*
sand sage *(Artemisia filifolia)*
silvery sophora *(Sophora stenophylla)*
Welsh's milkweed *(Asclepias welshii)*

Where to stay

Parry Lodge
89 East Center Street
Kanab, Utah
888-289-1722
www.parrylodge.com

Where to eat

The Junction Drive-Inn
Good thick Utah shakes that you eat with a spoon and lots of fried stuff. If you haven't had a Utah shake, don't miss the chance to try one—they are chunky and will make you chunky as well.
185 East 300 South
Kanab, Utah
435-644-8170

What to read

Dune Country: A Naturalist's Look at the Plant Life of Southwestern Sand Dunes, by Janice Emily Bowers. University of Arizona Press, 1998.

Mormon Country, by Wallace Stegner. Bison Books, 2003 (second edition).

. . . .

The ubiquitous rough mules ears—king of the dunes.

Sizing Up the Big Boojum: Baja California

When: *late March, 2006*
Destination: *Baja California, Mexico*
Total trip time: *6 days*
Vehicle: *2000 Toyota 4Runner with 115,000 miles*
Roundtrip distance from Tucson: *1,600 miles*
Traveling companions: *Dan Weber and Simmons Buntin*
Music: *soundtrack to the film* The Life Aquatic *(mainly the David Bowie covers by Seu Jorge)*

RESEARCH FOR MY TRIP TO BAJA BEGAN, of all places, in Manhattan, on a rainy October afternoon the year before at the New York Public Library. While looking at an exhibition called *Treasured Maps: Celebrating the Lionel Pincus and Princess Firyal Map Division*, I came across a mysterious map from 1686 London, titled "A New Mapp of the World." For me, the most curious feature of the map was that California was depicted as an island. The literature that accompanied the map suggested that the mistake was made as the "result of unfamiliarity or poor communication." What the cartographer's error brought to my mind was Bruce Berger's book about Baja California, titled *Almost an Island*, which I had recently read with relish, and which suggested that in many respects, Baja remains as strange and isolated as an island. It whetted my appetite for Baja, a region of the Sonoran Desert that I had never visited.

As it became apparent that the crackling dry winter of 2006 would not yield the rivers of wildflowers we had hoped for, I turned my attention to a preposterous plant native to the Mexican states of Sonora and Baja California: the boojum tree (*Fouquieria columnaris*). I pondered over this gigantic pylon-shaped plant that shoots up from

A desert rat's version of a drive through Redwood National Forest: Baja's boojum-filled Montevideo Canyon.

the ground like a sage-green upside-down parsnip. I was not searching for just any boojum, but rather, for the largest boojum on the planet. On account of the dry year, we would most likely not be fording great rivers of lupine or happening across valleys of poppies; on the other hand, finding a singularly exclamatory boojum, the greatest plant of its kind on earth, seemed like more than sufficient justification for the trip.

I had seen boojums in cultivation and read Richard Felger's stylish description of this plant: "Looking like great upturned carrots with scraggly little secondary branches, the boojum is one of the most unusual plants in the world."

Curvaceous boojums near Cataviña.

Technically they are a stem succulent, but they are included in Richard Felger's *Trees of Sonora*, in part because they are big enough to climb. Some time in the early 1900s, when Godfrey Sykes first sighted these strange plants, he announced, "Ho, ho, a Boojum. Yes, definitely a Boojum." Sykes was referring to the Lewis Carroll poem, "The Hunting of the Snark."

But if ever I meet with a Boojum, that day,
In a moment (of this I am sure),
I shall softly and suddenly vanish away—
And the notion I cannot endure!

The author Susan Lowell, who happens to be the great-granddaughter of Godfrey Sykes, told me that he called the young plants "boojum treelets"; later, reading Sykes's *A Westerly Trend*, I learned that Sykes also called a lot of the small towns in the West "townlets." This fantastic Seussian portrait of the boojum and its associates egged me on, and I recruited two friends for the adventure that would take us 1,600 miles in an out-and-back journey into the heart of Baja's central deserts. Traveling with me was Simmons Buntin—poet, editor, and confirmed south-of-the-border troublemaker— and Dan Weber—a hydrogeologist, also known as "Science Man." Our vehicle, Dan Weber's 2000 Toyota 4Runner, had recently been purchased from a Navajo Indian couple who told Dan that the truck had been blessed by a medicine man. The 4Runner's bumper was plastered with a 2006 Denver Powwow sticker that advertised the dates of March 24, 25, and 26—eerily, the same dates we would be in Baja; we regarded both the medicine man's blessing and the bumper sticker as auspicious signs. We didn't have any dream catchers hanging from the rearview mirror, and none of us were wearing moccasins or silver jewelry, but when it came to trusting in the medicine man's blessing on the Toyota, we were like three white Navajos—Navahonkies, if you will.

We rolled out of Tucson before the crack of dawn on an adventure that felt a little like a hunting expedition—which, in fact, it was: we were out to bag a boojum. With no wives or girlfriends around to be disgusted or appalled at our convenience-store selections, we did as boys and young men have done throughout the ages and bought dried and pickled processed-meat products for en-route consumption. Our trip to Baja began with a stop at a Quik Mart in El Centro, California, to purchase several staple items for the journey, including a pickled sausage called Tijuana Mama, whose label promised "300% Hotter"—to which my first response was, "than what?" The Tijuana Mama, as it turned out, was quite hot, but thankfully I had also procured a sour-apple Abba Zabba, which is a peanut-butter-filled sour-apple taffy candy bar that is guaranteed to pull out loose fillings. The Abba Zabba proved a healing balm to my burning mouth.

As we got back into the car the last time before crossing into Mexico, Simmons, with his record of somewhat spastic border mishaps, appeared slightly nervous about crossing the line into Mexico. Simmons asked, "Are we going straight over the border now?" to which Dan replied, "Heart of darkness."

The first day of our trip took us across the border at the mountain town of Tecate, home of the Cervecería Cuauhtemoc Moctezuma brewery, which brews the burgundy-and-black-labeled Tecate beer so prevalent in northern Mexico—and according to author David Yetman, the beer of choice of Mexican drug *traficantes* driving newer-model Chevy pickups. We ate lunch beneath large ash trees (*Fraxinus veluntina*, or *fresnos* in Spanish) in the central plaza of the Parque Miguel Hidalgo, enjoying cold Tecates with excellent enchiladas and beef tacos. Then we drove south of Tecate through a lovely agricultural valley filled with grape vines and olive groves, finally reaching the busy and surprisingly Americanized Ensenada, complete with a newly opened Home Depot, Costco, and an Office Depot that would become important to us later in our trip.

Other than finding and measuring Baja's big boojum, the other high-priority goal on our trip was the gluttonous consumption of fish tacos. As we piloted the Toyota 4Runner south, we made a series of pacts that would guide us through Mexico: eat fish tacos twice daily, swim in both the Pacific Ocean and the Sea of Cortez, and wash down the previously mentioned fish tacos with beer brewed in the state of Baja California, or when that was not available, Mexican Coca-Cola in glass bottles. Besides the retro novelty of drinking Coke from bottles, Mexican Coca-Cola is made with cane sugar rather than the high-fructose corn-sweetener *du jour* found in its American cousin. I find the sweet Mexican version (though probably equally unhealthy) far superior. So much so that Zoë's Mexican pop-bottle collection, which contains several styles of glass Coke bottles, hangs proudly from our ramada and has become a fixture in our backyard garden. We also agreed to stop the car without complaint whenever we saw an interesting plant.

We had hoped to make it as far south as the beaches of San Quintín for our first night of

....

Sustenance for surfers and wildflower hunters alike: the baja fish taco, pictured here at Las Hamacas in Bahía de los Angelos.

camping, but we were distracted by a seductively bad road up a mountain canyon leading to the tiny agricultural and fishing *ejido* (a communal Mexican farming or fishing village) of Eréndira, and, more importantly, to the Eréndira Cocina Familiar, where we dined on the first fish tacos of our trip in a brightly painted red-and-white-plywood shack that would inform our tastes about all of the fish tacos we would eat in the week to come. The recipe for fish tacos in Baja varies from region to region. Usually, it is fresh fried fish served on soft corn tortillas and topped with mayonnaise, cabbage, and *pico de gallo*—a fresh salsa of tomatoes, onions, cilantro, jalapeños, and lime juice. Eréndira, which has its own little fishing fleet and is surrounded by cabbage and onion fields, proved the perfect place to be introduced to the Baja fish taco. The fish, which we were told was fresh dorado, was fried in a batter that could be compared only to fine Japanese tempura—crisp and light with a hint of beer

flavor. The cabbage and salsas were fresh and gratifying, and the corn tortillas warm and moist.

Our camp, ominously named "Malibu Beach," was perched on a little dirt bluff overlooking the ocean and surrounded by cabbage fields. With a name like that I half expected a Starbucks and California Pizza Kitchen to flank the campground. Thankfully, it was just us and a large Mexican family camped there. We slept to the rhythm of the churning Pacific twenty feet below. In the morning, we completed our first pact with a quick swim in the Pacific, which to be sure was still quite cold. I entered first on a sandy portion of beach, after which Simmons and Dan unwisely choose a gravelly spit with an undertow that upended them, resulting in some raspberry scratches on the legs of Buntin and Science Man. Their wounds were minor and failed to draw blood or much sympathy but nevertheless gave both of them reasons to complain about our pact and my insistence on swimming in the Pacific for much of the rest of the trip.

On a cloudy Sunday morning we pulled out of Eréndira to begin the serious plant-hunting portion of our trip. We were scarcely back on the bad road toward the trans-peninsular highway when we were detained by a flock of turkeys and the appearance of blooming flattop buckwheat (*Eriogonum fasciculatum*) by the roadside. In classic Simmons-Mexico fashion, we parked the car right on the roadway and began to photograph the pinky-white umbrella-shaped flowers that resembled a deserty version of yarrow or maybe Queen Anne's lace. As we hunkered down on the disturbed roadside, other jewels became apparent—a pattern that repeated itself throughout the rest of our trip.

Baja is filled with rarities and curiosities. Near the buckwheat, we found several chalk lettuce (*Dudleya brittoniana*, also known as chalk dudleya) and many San Diego sunflowers (*Viguiera deltoidea*). The dudleya is a twist on other familiar succulents like echeveria and sempervium; their rosette shape also recalls a barbless agave. We took pictures and got back on the road.

The 4Runner bounced through the long mercado strip of San Quintín and up into the mountains to El Rosario, where we made a mandatory stop for fish tacos at a cabaña-type restaurant that had a Mexican bus parked out front. Simmons, with his Boris Becker resemblance and 6'5" stature, had thus far managed a fair amount of cultural sensitivity on this trip. He had not had any major burrito blowouts or knocked over any large point-of-purchase Tic-Tac displays. Just as I was beginning to think that Simmons had finally slipped into a Mexico state of mind, he did the unthinkable in Cocina Rosarita. We had been served the delicious cane-sugar Mexican Coca-Cola in bottles and were awaiting our fish tacos, when Simmons stood up, waltzed across the restaurant, stepped behind the cash register, and unplugged an electronic singing *trucha* (trout) that was belting out the Manfred Mann classic "Do wah diddy diddy dum diddy do" while it hung on the wall. Just as the trout was beginning another round with "Here she comes just a walking down the street," the trucha went silent and all of the patrons and staff of the restaurant, including

The pleasures of camping on the Pacific coast of Baja.

Chalk dudleya found beside the trans-peninsular highway north of Cataviña.

Dan and me, looked at Simmons in disbelief. A giant American had taken away the do wah diddy. Everyone knows that a singing trout is the international symbol of good times and good fun. Dan and I hung our heads as we finished off our fish tacos and quickly exited the café, pretending not to know Simmons very well.

Climbing the coastal range toward the drier midsection of the peninsula, we approached the most botanically weird area in North America; if you like your plants on the kinky side, Baja's central desert is the place to go. We began to see ghostly white chalk dudleya growing out of the road cuts. A short time later, we spied our first boojum, covered in ball moss (*Tillandsia recurvata*) and looking quite bent over and forlorn. It had that look of a plant that was closer to the cold Pacific than it wanted to be. If boojums could talk, I imagined that this one would have said, "Give me heat."

A little coastal fog was still burning off over the valley, but as it dissipated, what I saw gave me chills of excitement and made the hair on the back of my neck stand up: a granite-boulder-filled valley guarded by what looked like millions of flagpole-like boojums and the seemingly more civilized cardóns (*Pachycereus pringlei*), defying gravity and logic. The cardón, a bombastic pillar-like cactus that presides over the Baja desert, is often mistaken for its more northerly cousin, the saguaro, but if you look closely, the cardón's skin has a blue cast, with gray stripes along its ribs that look a little like pinstripes. Not a dainty plant, the cardón's beefy trunk can swell to a diameter of over six feet while its phallic arms can soar to over seventy feet high. Entering Cataviña was a thrill; the term "otherworldly" was used. As we entered Cataviña, which was no more than a little store and gas station wedged between boulders, my iPod, which we had plugged into the car stereo, eerily switched to a Portuguese cover of the David Bowie song "Life on Mars?" by the Brazilian singer Seu Jorge. The song fit our mood excellently. The 4Runner seemed to have temporarily transformed itself into a lunar lander, crawling over the surface of a foreign planet.

We stayed the night in a quiet little campground on the grounds of the ranch at San Isidro, just outside Cataviña. We arrived in the afternoon, and after quickly pitching our tents we began jumping boulder-to-boulder with our cameras, making the best of the evening light.

Deep in the boulders of the Cataviña wilderness, there is no denying that you are in a forest. Not only boojums, but giant blue-green cardóns tower over you, and growing from impossible cracks in the rocks, the fat white papery trunks of elephant trees stake their claim. Down beneath the boojums was another highly sought-after Arizona landscape plant, the spectacular fire barrel or *bisnaga colorada* (*Ferocactus gracilis*) with its curved red spines, growing freely in this rare Baja wilderness. The genus name, *Ferocactus*, is derived from the word "ferocious," and all of the barrel cacti in that genus are notoriously tough. I love these fire barrels and was tempted by them for much of the trip. Because Simmons and Dan knew my weakness, they kept pointing out beautiful little specimens with long candy-apple-red spines that could be popped out of the ground with nothing more than a Bic pen, stowed in a backpack, and smuggled back across the border. But besides the fact that it goes against my personal ethics to take plants from the wild, I knew we would have to pass through several more Mexican army checkpoints on the way back; I had no idea how much a bribe for a smuggled fire barrel would set me back and didn't want to find out. Also, I had no desire to find myself in a Mexican jail explaining to my fellow prisoners, "*Hermanos,* I am here because I fell in love with a ferocious cactus, *¿comprende?*"

You can imagine my alarm when, after my torturous ethical deliberations, I flipped open Norman Roberts's Baja California field guide to a photo captioned, "Biznaga being fed to pigs at Bahía de los Angeles." Adding insult to injury, the accompanying paragraph went on to explain that "during periods of drought severe enough to reduce forage, these cacti are cut down and split or sometimes doused with kerosene and set aflame to burn the spines, then chopped up to feed livestock." Perhaps taking a bisnaga (biznaga) home would save it from a fiery and hoggy death—still, I had my principles (and the threat of Mexican prison) to keep our vehicle bisnaga-free on the trip back over the frontera.

After climbing to the top of a fin-like granite escarpment and setting up my tripod, I suddenly noticed I was not alone. A caveat about Mexican travel that seems to hold true is that no matter how far you are from civilization, you are never far from a stray dog. Staring pitifully at me with its head slightly cocked was a medium-sized black and brown dog with semi-floppy ears who had somehow followed me up the boulder fin. I had nothing to feed him, not even a Tijuana Mama sausage wrapper for him to lick; nevertheless, the pooch, who I nicknamed Perro Roca ("Rock Dog") continued to bird-dog me, although somewhat warily.

I loved hopping from boulder to boulder among boojums and cardóns. I was a tall skinny guy in a forest of tall skinny plants, and I felt right at home. Being in the thick of this thorny and succulent forest had me feeling ecstatic. I found a quote in a Valle de los Cirios pamphlet in which the well-known Baja flora enthusiast Robert R. Humphrey called this central portion of Baja "the most rich and interesting variety of plants of all the deserts in the world." It was too much to take in before dark, and so we reluctantly headed back to the ranch house, where we had a fine, if slightly greasy, dinner of hard-shell beef tacos under a *palapa* (a rustic shade structure) of palm fronds at the ranch headquarters before turning in for the night.

In the morning Simmons and I got up before sunrise, eager to see as much of the surrounding flora as we could before midday. As we sometimes do, Simmons went one direction, and I the other. I hiked up a hill near a small airstrip behind the ranch, where I photographed twenty-foot-high elephant trees with trunks so white and fat and undulating that they reminded me of the porcelain-white thighs of a carnival fat lady. Well, on account of the elephant tree's peeling bark, maybe it more closely resembled a carnival fat lady recovering from sunburn. In either case, the early, translucent robin's-egg-blue light of morning, a shade that as far as I know is found only in the desert sky, made a fine backdrop for the white trunks of the elephant trees.

While the air was still cool, I explored a large sandy arroyo peppered with boulders; I was struck by the icy grandeur of the Mexican blue palms (*Brahea armata*) which in some cases appeared to grow directly out of large boulders strewn across the arroyo. As a desert-garden designer, it has

An elephant tree at dawn in Cataviña.

taken me a number of years to warm up to palm trees. In urban landscapes they often smack of the kind of water-intensive blandness that used to be employed around resorts. It also seemed that palms were sometimes used as a symbol to would-be residents saying, "Move on in; as you can see from our palm trees, we are an oasis with plenty of water for all comers." But the Mexican blue palm, ah, the sweet, cool, icy-blue palm; it was a palm I could get behind. I had planted Mexican palms in some of the Arizona gardens I'd designed, but I'd never seen specimens like these in Cataviña. The largest, which had to be quite old, approached thirty feet in height. One of the reasons the Mexican blue palm is such a good choice for residential gardens is that it stays relatively small and is very cold-hardy, withstanding cold snaps into the high teens. Down among the rocks, I also spotted Baja fairy duster (*Calliandra californica*), an enormously popular desert landscaping plant and hummingbird attractor in Arizona. Seeing it in the wild made me grin.

After turning off the trans-peninsular highway toward Bahía de los Angeles ("Bay of the Angels"), we entered the Valle de los Cirios in earnest (*valle* means valley, and *cirio*, which means wax candle, is also the Spanish name for the boojum tree). Some might consider this lush desert of freakishly tall succulent plants, big rocky vistas, and the occasional venomous reptile as vastly intimidating; on the contrary, we embraced the landscape as long-lost brother to our northern Sonoran haunts. I thought about the uneasiness and near claustrophobia I had felt my first time in a great hardwood forest of the eastern U.S.—a discomfort I later attributed to the lack of transparency to the landscape—and I was overjoyed to be out in the transparent clear air, massive rock mountains, and thorny plants of Baja. As we pulled off the road for a pee break under a big blue sky, we were unprepared for horticultural discovery. I spied the sky-blue flowers and silver leaves of Sonoran nightshade (*Solanum hindsianum*) flourishing just beside the roadway. Not four steps off the highway, I encountered one of my favorite garden plants— one I'd never seen growing in the wild—the slipper plant (*Pedilanthus macrocarpus*). With its gray-green snakelike stems, the plant appears a bit like medusa's hair, but it gets its name from its flowers, which resemble a woman's high-heeled shoe. The slipper plant has become the sweetheart of desert-landscape designers and can be found in front of many upscale contemporary homes in Scottsdale and Tucson. There is no denying the sexy nature of the plant, although I would argue that the slipper plant has a confused sexual identity: its turgid upright stems are most certainly phallic, while its flowers are so delicate that they seem to dangle like pendants on a necklace, enticing passing hummingbirds. The fruit that follows the flower looks like a swollen heart ready to break—a chubby locket with a photo of your true love inside. No wonder the slipper plant is everyone's sweetheart, even if it can't decide if it is a girl or boy.

Arriving in Bahía de los Angeles mid-morning, we stopped at Dagget's Campground, a tidy beachside waypoint that offered us our own shade *palapa* and a fire ring made from the steel drum of a discarded washing machine. After pitching our tents and getting the lay of the land, we snorkeled in the warmer and less choppy Sea of Cortez, spotting rock bass along the stony bottom. The bottom of the sea looked like the same rocky landscape minus cacti, trees, and flowers.

Thanks to our swim, we arrived back on shore famished and decided to venture into town to investigate the fish-taco situation and check with the local authorities about the exact location of the road to the big boojum. We stopped in a general store next door to a tourist office in the middle of town. The tourist office was dark inside, and the door was locked. After inquiring in the general store, we learned two important facts: there was a local office of the National Commission of Protected Areas that could help us with boojum directions, and the best fish tacos in town were at Las Hamacas ("the hammocks") restaurant. Not only did we get directions to these important places, an animated sanitation manager (i.e. garbage-truck driver) offered to escort us. "Follow me," he said in Spanish, making a big arm gesture. Hopping back in the 4Runner, we soon found ourselves following a beat-up orange school bus stuffed with trash, with a back door that flapped open and closed, toward the best fish tacos in Bahía de los Angeles. We chuckled as we considered the wisdom of taking restaurant recommendations from a garbage man who didn't even have a real garbage truck. But I remembered that the legendary food writer Calvin Trilling had commented that for travelers in a strange city, the worst restaurant recommendations were likely to come from chamber of commerce boosters, who were likely to recommend rotating restaurants on the tops of skyscrapers— but salty restaurant recommendations from garbage men…those were bound to be authentic. Our hunch was correct, and from the exquisite fresh blender salsa, to the hot *tortillas de harina* (flour tortillas), the meal was superb and different from the fish tacos we had on the Pacific side of the peninsula. Although I was initially suspicious of the flour tortillas, their softer texture offered a fresh take on a pervasive peninsular dish. The breading on the fish was also darker than on the fish we had on the Pacific side of Baja (perhaps it was beer-battered). Making a quick stop at the Protected Areas office, we got better directions to the canyon we would visit in the evening.

As the afternoon light turned golden, we entered the mouth of Montevideo Canyon. Putting the 4Runner into low gear, we muscled through the sandy washes, narrowly avoiding a giant *datillo* or tree yucca (*Yucca valida*, also sometimes called datil yucca) that had fallen over the road. The canyon constricted, and the road passed a rocky outcrop dotted with elephant trees. This area, part of the larger protected area known as Valle de los Cirios, is unique. Whether it is the canyon's sandy soil or the wind protection it offers is hard to say, but what *can* be said is that this valley is full of giants. The cardóns and the boojums that grow here are the biggest in the world, some reaching heights of over sixty feet, or to use the parlance of Science Man, ten Simmons. We were awestruck, and in the glowing light, we felt as though we were in the presence of ancients. This was the desert equivalent of a trip deep into an old-growth forest of redwoods or sequoias. The 4Runner was dwarfed by the massive boojums, which grew so near the road that driving was a slow threading of the needle. Back in Tucson, Gene Joseph, the noted nurseryman and Baja aficionado, had given me directions to the big boojum, telling us the approximate mileage and which side of the road to look. He had warned

me, "You would think that it would be easy to spot, but it is in the midst of a lot of really big boojums and cardóns." As we wound our way through the valley this proved true. Our eyes were glued to the landscape, scanning the horizons for that one plant that stood out from the rest. We had several false positives. "Wait," we would say, "look at that one … it's a big mother … but I don't know." We had all the windows down and from time to time, one of us would stick his head out of the sunroof for a clearer view. Being in this canyon, at this time of evening, seemed to us much like hunting for the elusive snark:

> Each thought he was thinking of nothing
> but "Snark"
> And the glorious work of the day;
> And each tried to pretend that he did not
> remark
> That the other was going that way.
>
> But the valley grew narrow and narrower
> still,
> And the evening got darker and colder,
> Till (merely from nervousness, not from
> goodwill)
> They marched along shoulder to shoulder.
> (*from "The Hunting of the Snark"*
> *by Lewis Carroll*)

Finally, as we came around a bend, we spotted it. It was clearly larger than anything we had seen up to this point. I also recognized the slight curvature near the top from a picture on the cover of a back issue of *Desert Plants* magazine. We hiked in about a hundred yards off the road toward the big boojum in silence. Growing next to it was an enormous cardón, and they stood together like a couple of old sages having a long discussion. Dumbstruck, we walked right up underneath the big boojum. We walked all around it in circles, looked at it from every side, walked one hundred yards away, and squinted up toward the top. After standing there for a while I took pictures: a close-up of the leaves, a shot with Simmons holding a ten-foot tape measure for scale reference, long shots capturing the whole plant—which proved impossible. It was not that I couldn't frame the entire plant in my lens, but that the massive ancient presence of the big boojum was something that was best experienced in person. We shot pictures until our light was nearly gone and then drove back to some pictographs at the back of the canyon, backtracking to check our mileage. When you look closely at the trunk of a boojum, it is gnarly, like pale-green cork, with dark-gray polka dots where its branchlets originate. There is something about the plant that lends an appearance of fragility, belying its massive size and drought tolerance. Perhaps this is what Godfrey Sykes inferred when he tenderly referred to the juveniles as "treelets." Compared with their close relative the ocotillo, the boojum is downright anthropomorphic—maybe because of its torso-like trunk. The ocotillo, on the other hand, with its thorny canes that zigzag like lightning, appears merciless.

Around the campfire that night in L.A. Bay, the true brilliance of the washtub fire ring shone through; our little fire thrived in the enclosure, sending out striking pinpricks of light through its perforated sides. We sat around the fire drinking Cerveza Tijuana, or "T.J." beer, and talking about the big boojum. Dan Weber burned a couple of dead elephant-tree twigs that he had found on the

ground in Cataviña, which released a perfumed incense as the resinous sap smoked. As I was enjoying the evening under the rustic ramada, I thought out loud, "This is all anyone needs in a garden. We have a rustic and stylish palapa for shade, a handsome washer-drum fire for warmth, coolers to sit on, and a landscape of sculptural plants surrounding us." I get some of my best garden-design ideas from Mexican taco stands,

The author, Dan Weber, and el cirio mas grande del mundo.

bus stops, and campsites. I vowed to find some washing-machine tubs to use as fire pits in the next garden I designed. The topic turned to the actual height of the boojum. We had been so disoriented by the general majesty of the plant and its setting that we hadn't really taken the time to properly calculate the height. Using Simmons as a measure, Dan had squinted and held up a pencil, roughly figuring that it was eleven Simmonses high. But to Dan and me, the "Simmons Method" didn't seem very scientific, and I was counting on my pictures with the tape measure to calculate the height back at home. Simmons mentioned that my lens would distort and curve the image, making it nearly impossible to correctly figure the height. Thankfully, Science Man suggested that we could figure that height using junior-high geometry, if we just took more measurements. We decided to return the next morning.

Using two tripods, an Easton 7075 aluminum tent pole, and a long rope for measuring, we used the geometry of similar triangles to make a drawing on notebook paper of the distances involved. Using the tent pole as a sight, I located the top, and Dan and I worked to take measurements on a note pad while Simmons wandered around like a big impatient kid asking if we were ready to go yet. He was interested in the plant, but our tedious measurements were almost more than he could bear. After taking all of the measurements we could, we said goodbye to our tall friend (the boojum, not Simmons) and headed out on the rough dirt road to the Spanish mission at San Borja.

Our mood was celebratory on the way back toward *el norte*. Along the *mercado* strip of San Quintín, we stopped and bought a bag of fresh-roasted garbanzo beans garnished with salsa. To wash down the 'banzos, I mixed *micheladas* in the back seat (Mexican beer, lime juice, and Clamato juice) for Dan and myself while Simmons drove. We estimated the height of the boojum as somewhere between eighty-five and ninety-one feet high. Matt Johnson, the noted Sonoran horticulturist, told me that in 1981, when he first visited the big boojum, he had estimated its height at eighty-one feet. To verify our calculations, Dan informed us that we would need a scientific calculator with a tangent function. The words "scientific calculator" and "tangent function" used together drew a collective Homer Simpson-style "Huh?" from Simmons and me. Although I didn't know much about using a scientific calculator, I did know where to find one. As I previously mentioned, we had passed a large Office Max in Ensenada on our way down. We stopped and hurriedly went back to the calculator aisle, where Dan punched our numbers into a still-in-the-plastic-packaging HP model, which spit out the number 91 feet. The big boojum—giant, turgid, tapered, and rising from the desert floor—had made a big impression. Finding the big boojum, in this valley of giants, was a story for the grandchildren.

After returning to Tucson, I read something that made our journey seem even more improbable. In a chapter on the ocotillo family (Fouquieriacae) in *A Natural History of the Sonoran Desert*, Mark Dimmitt had written that "The tallest known boojum was discovered by Robert Humphrey in Montevideo Canyon near Bahia de los Angeles in the 1970s; at the time it was 81 feet (24.6 m) tall. It grew several more feet in the next 20 years. In

1998 it [the big boojum] and the 60-foot-tall cardón next to it were gone, probably casualties of Hurricane Nora which crossed that part of the peninsula in September of 1997. We could not find any boojums over 50 feet (15 m) tall in that canyon in 1998." It appeared that Simmons, Science Man, and I had found a plant that wasn't even supposed to be there anymore. I e-mailed Mark for clarification, to which he replied, "I was unable to find the plant in 1998, probably due to the lush growth during that very wet year, and we did find many downed large trees. But I did relocate it in 2001. I corrected the error on the Desert Museum's website, but, alas, books are not so easily corrected." I liked that fact that for about three years the big boojum pulled a disappearing act, and to me, the boojum resurrection only added to the shroud of mystery around this venerable and wily giant.

• •

Plants to find

Baja fairy duster *(Calliandra californica)*
ball moss *(Tillandsia recurvata)*
boojum or cirio *(Fouquieria columnaris)*
cardón *(Pachycereus pringlei)*
chalk dudleya, chalk lettuce, dudleya *(Dudleya brittoniana)*
coastal agave *(Agave shawii)*
datil yucca, datillo, tree yucca *(Yucca valida)*
elephant tree *(Bursera microphylla)*
fire barrel or bisnaga colorada *(Ferocactus gracilis)*
flattop buckwheat *(Eriogonum fasciculatum)*
Mexican blue palm *(Brahea armata)*
Mexican tree ocotillo *(Fouquieria macdougallii)*
Our Lord's candle *(Yucca whipplei)*
San Diego sunflower *(Viguiera deltoidea)*
senita cactus *(Lophocereus schottii)*
slipper plant *(Pedilanthus macrocarpus)*
Sonoran nightshade *(Solanum hindsianum)*

Where to camp

Buy the guide called *Baja Camping,* by Fred and Gloria Jones, which will give you many camping options on the peninsula; so if you don't make it where you're headed, you'll have other choices.

Where to eat

This is a tiny sample of the stands that line the roads. Most don't have telephones or addresses. Try any place that is crowded with locals.
Cocina Familiar in Eréndira
Las Hamacas in Bahía de los Angeles
Cocina Rosarita in El Rosario

What to read

Almost an Island: Travels in Baja California, by Bruce Berger. University of Arizona Press, 1998.
The Annotated Hunting of the Snark, by Lewis Carroll, edited with annotations by Martin Gardner. W. W. Norton, 2006.
Baja California Plant Field Guide, by Norman C. Roberts. Natural History Publishing Co., 1989.
A Natural History of the Sonoran Desert, by Stephen Phillips and Patricia Wentworth Comus, editors. Arizona-Sonora Desert Museum Press and University of California Press, 2000.
The Trees of Sonora, Mexico, by Richard Stephen Felger, Matthew Brian Johnson, and Michael Francis Wilson. Oxford University Press, 2001.

A Lake of Pure Sunshine: California

When: *early April 2006*
Destination: *Lancaster, California*
Total trip time: *3 days*
Vehicle: *1999 VW Jetta TDI*
Roundtrip distance from Tucson: *1,060 miles*
Traveling solo
Music: *The Beach Boys'* Smiley Smile; *My Morning Jacket's* It Still Moves;
Mason Jennings's self-titled album

WHEN I ASKED MY FRIEND Darrell Hussman, who grew up in Lancaster, California, about his hometown, he said, "The weather is just like Tucson's but the wind blows 30 miles an hour all the time and they don't get any rain in the summer. All of the friends I grew up with there have left except those who are addicted to drugs. It's a crime-ridden bedroom community of Los Angeles. I haven't been back in years."

"What about the California Poppy Reserve?" I asked.

"Now that," replied Darrell, "is freaking amazing! I remember going out there past fields full of

The rainbow-graced, but nearly poppy-free, California Poppy Reserve in 2006.

tumbleweeds and seeing this enormous sea of orange—orange like an enormous pumpkin patch. It's a fabulous place."

For many Western wildflower hunters, Antelope Valley California Poppy Reserve is mecca. Naturalists have long recognized the special qualities of the place, situated at the southern end of California's massive central valley. Nearly a century ago, John Muir wrote what now seems a little like an epitaph, since much of this five-hundred-mile-long valley has been plowed under for agriculture or developed:

One shining morning a landscape was revealed that after all my wanderings still appears the most beautiful I have ever beheld. At my feet lay the Great Valley of California, level and flowery, like a lake of pure sunshine forty or fifty miles wide, five hundred miles long, one rich furred garden of yellow Compositae.

On this first wildflower-chasing trip over to California, I wasn't really planning on heading out to Antelope Valley to see wildflowers. The naysayers had nearly convinced me that the dry winter had nixed all hope for California wildflower fabulosity in 2006.

I had just spent several days in north San Diego County, scouting for garden photos, and I was a little road weary. I decided to grab a bite to eat and then head for home. I stopped at a Panera café in Carlsbad to check my e-mail and eat a *panino*. Out of habit, I checked out the Desert USA's wildflower-watch website, not expecting to find any great reports. I recalled that some big Pacific storms had recently dumped rain north of Los Angeles, but how far north? I soon discovered that on April 8, someone had posted pictures of goldfields (*Lasthenia californica*) and California poppies (*Eschscholtzia californica*) blooming at an intersection near the Antelope Valley reserve—vivid yellows and oranges—on the website. I checked the date; it was April 10. All of a sudden, I had the fever: no, I would not be going home. I got in the Jetta, cut over to I-15 and pointed her north. I was determined to be standing in Antelope Valley taking pictures that day in good evening light. Even Darrell's description of the harsh climate and tough reputation of Lancaster egged me on. In fact, there is a relationship between desolate-looking landscapes and good

mass-wildflower shows. Mark Dimmitt writes that "the more arid the habitat, the greater proportion of annual species in North America… In the driest habitats, such as the sandy flats near Yuma, Arizona, up to ninety percent of the plants are annuals." So that is why when the Algodones Dunes near Yuma bloom, they can get choked with royal purple sand verbena and spikes of Ajo lily—they have no competition.

The San Gabriel Mountains are the only thing keeping L.A. from running up hard against Lancaster. From I-15, I cut over to Palmdale on Highway 138, which is also known as the Pearblossom Highway. The highway follows the northern foothills of the San Gabriels and, as billed, orchards of carefully pruned pear trees line sections of the road; more interesting to me were Joshua-tree badlands interspersed with the pear quadrants—pears and giant yuccas make strange bedfellows indeed, I thought. I've made no secret of my love for agaves, yuccas, and other lily-family plants, so when I came across an excerpt from *Joshua Tree: Desolation Tango*, by Deanne Stillman, I thought her description of the big yucca was perfectly articulated:

The Joshua tree had me at hello. It was beautiful, weird, and freaky all at once. With its daggered desert armor it seemed to be sending out and receiving messages all the time—or maybe it just looked that way. Whatever it was doing, I liked it, and it liked me. "It's okay to dream," it told me, "really!"

When I turned north onto Highway 14, the roadside yuccas petered out, and Lancaster arose like a dusty and forgotten province of L.A. I stopped only for gas, then hurried out to the poppy preserve, which—as it turns out—is some distance out of town. All afternoon, the weather had threatened. Dark-gray clouds had gathered over the mountains and valleys, looking a lot like rain. I reached the edge of the poppy preserve as big, low, blousy clouds crept over the hills. Then I saw it—down between the gray clumps of rabbit-brush (*Ericameria nauseosa*) was a carpet of gold-fields, a tiny yellow daisy that sends up 500 to 800 blooms per square foot! The clumps of rabbit-brush, a plant I knew from Utah's Great Basin, reminded me that I was in the colder Mojave Desert, a place that could top the statue-of-liberty-like Joshua tree spikes with crowns of

snow. I pulled over, jumped out, and started snapping photos just as a light rain began to fall. I drove a bit farther west on a dirt road toward some hills covered in gold streaks, with giant Joshua trees in the foreground. When the road got too steep and muddy for the Jetta, I pulled on my favorite Picacho Peak hoodie, featuring a silk-screened silhouette of the Arizona peak renowned for its Mexican gold poppy displays, and started hiking, distracted by the lovely Joshua trees (*Yucca brevifolia*), who seemed to me like friendly roadside oracles on this stormy evening. I love Joshua trees; these Shaquille O'Neals of the Yucca family can reach heights of fifty feet. They are monumental, and as much as any other desert

Joshua trees and goldfields on a misty evening.

Joshua tree bloom above a goldfield carpet.

plants, including the boojums we saw in Baja, they recall modern art. Joshua trees—in a fashion that would please the late great British gardener Sir Christopher Lloyd, who liked his gardens "shaggy"—have a disheveled look resulting from the skirts of dried leaves that cling to their trunks. Although their size reminds me of Shaq, their posture is more Keith Richards. Their curving trunks and spiked leaves have a hip, ancient quality and seem to say, "I've had a long night, sweethearts, but I've managed to send up these fabulous bayonets for your enjoyment. God, I need a nap." I remembered driving through the yuccaless dunes of the Pinacate in March of 2005 with Simmons,

listening to U2's *Joshua Tree* album, but here was where I needed that soundtrack! The Joshuas were blooming, and their pink-and-cream stalks kept me company as I walked. I walked by a pretty Cooper's goldenbush (*Ericameria cooperi*) beside a zigzag barbed-wire fence, and then on a little sandy bank I found an architecturally thorny blue flower I didn't know. Its silvery leaves and stem looked like a thistle, but the shape of the flowers was sagelike. Was it a sage or a thistle? When I looked it up, it turned out to be both. Technically, it was a sage (*Salvia carduacea*), but its common name, thistle sage, is a nod to its well-armed resemblance. On the same hillside, chia (*Salvia columbariae*), with its purple-blue whorls, was also in bloom. The protein-rich seeds of both of the above-mentioned salvias were important food plants for many Southwest Indian tribes, who would collect, roast, and grind the seeds to mix with water and sugar (possibly derived from a local cane grass). One story suggests that Mojave runners would make the trip from Needles, California, to the Pacific coast, fueled by nothing more than a mush of chia seeds and water.

After photographing the thistle sage and chia, I was losing my light quickly and glanced out at the valley in the distance. At the base of the mountains, I noticed a large swath of orange, as if a blimp filled with orange latex paint had gone down. "Ah ha!" I thought, "here is my destination for tomorrow." I stood stock-still in the dying light to take one more photo of Joshua trees with a goldfields background.

Wet, bone-tired, and hungry as a bear, I drove back into Lancaster to find sustenance. I looked around, trying to read the town. At first glance, the city did not impress. Like some of the worst development in Arizona, Lancaster had its share of semi-derelict strip malls and lots of "chain" everything—motels, restaurants, electronics stores—you name it. Luckily, I wasn't concerned with amenities, I was focused on wildflowers. When it comes to culture, Lancaster is kind of the opposite of Vail, Colorado, and I don't mean that in a completely negative way. I mean, Lancaster, like my home base of Tucson, is a real town where real working people live. But even more so than Tucson, Lancaster is not a place that puts on airs—it is what it is. It is a place where immigrants can settle and get a foothold. This is not a cappuccino-sipping, white wine kind of town. It is a down-to-earth city where in an old downtown you can find really good Salvadoran food—exactly what I found at a family-run place called Teclena Flores. Although it was late, the place was bustling with Salvadorans. I got a comfy vinyl booth and enjoyed a big plate of *Chuletas de Puerco Asadas* (grilled pork chops) with fresh salsa, plump *gorditas*, and a bottle of super-sweet golden Salvadoran soda pop that tasted like the essence of bubblegum. While I ate, families watched the news about President Bush's latest immigration-reform plan, with what to me looked like a vested interest. Whatever we do about immigration in this country, I'm sure about one thing, we should not keep people out who want come here to start good restaurants like Teclena Flores.

I pulled into the Motel 6, checked in, and slept until I was awakened by hip-hop music about 2:00 a.m. Evidently, there was a party around the pool that I hadn't been invited to. During my quest for wildflowers, I've spent a lot of nights at different Motel 6s in the West, and I've become adept at reading them. Although they claim the "no surprises" homogeneity of a big corporate chain, there are, in fact, surprises. The hackneyed real estate axiom—location, location, location—also holds true for the Motel 6. If the place is in a dicey urban neighborhood, especially on weekends, you're in for a house party or worse. If the place is all by its lonesome out on the Interstate and has a big parking lot, it will be filled with truckers and their attendant vices (Motel 6 walls are not well-insulated). How anyone can have an affair, or even a one-night stand, in a Motel 6 is beyond me. I honestly can't think of anything that would kill romance faster than swinging open the door to a Motel 6 room; there is really no amount of scented candles, soft music, and even good wine that could bring an amorous mood to a Motel 6 room. Anyway you serve it, a tryst in the 6 would feel more like a conjugal visit than a sensuous weekend. I've noticed that it's mostly lonely men who frequent the 6—truckers on the long haul, cheap traveling salesmen, tight writers, and wildflower photographers.

If the manager boasts about twenty-four-hour security cameras in the parking lot, you may want to reconsider. Also, a nonsmoking room in a Motel 6 means that they turn the ashtray on the nightstand over for you, and generally, but not always, the nonsmoking rooms will not have cigarette burns in the bedspreads. Perhaps Tom Bodett should record a new slogan for Motel 6; instead of "We'll leave the light on for you," it should be "We'll turn the ashtray over for you." In some "nonsmoking" rooms you'll wake up smelling like you've spent a long night in a Las Vegas casino. Never accept a room for the handicapped (I won't go into details here), and as Michael and Jane Stern emphatically note in their book *Two for the Road*, never, ever touch the polyester bedspread!

All in all, the Holiday Inn Express, if available, is usually about $20–$30 a night more than a Motel 6, but can feel much more luxurious (in the budget hotel category) even if just for the high-speed Internet connection.

So why *do* I stay at Motel 6s? First, I'm cheap, and I'd rather spend my money on a great meal than an expensive hotel; second, Motel 6s are everywhere and they publish a free directory listing all of the Motel 6s in the U.S. (which I keep in the car); third, in really upscale places, like Carpinteria near Santa Barbara, they can be the only cheap deal in town.

About the time the 50 Cent music died down and the kids around the pool turned in, I was up and dressed and out the door, headed back toward the big splotch of poppies I'd sighted the previous evening in Antelope Valley. Just before dawn, I had my tripod positioned in a lush field of flowers whose petals had closed for the night—but just before the light got good, steady rain began to fall. I waited around in the car, but it didn't seem that it would be clearing soon. I retreated to the Wee Vill Market, a little country store and café where I had a really good Spanish omelet and fresh hash browns. When the proprietor of the Wee Vill found out I was there for the wildflowers and that I had driven out from Tucson, she sweetly said, "Now Honey, next time you just call me and I'll tell you when the flowers are blooming, lots of folks do," and with that she wrote down the phone number and hours of the Wee Vill Market on a napkin for me. This woman struck me as the kind of self-reliant female who could run a whole town if they let her; she was the cook, the waitress, and the cashier, and the lines on her face looked like they ended up there from smiling and being in the sun. I read a freebie local paper in the Wee Vill for about an hour until the rain stopped, and then I was back out in the flowers.

I happened on a field of orange California poppies growing with a big, red wiry Brillo pad-like plant that I couldn't identify. It had the prodigious habit of an exotic invader, possibly from the mustard family, but I couldn't be sure; it also looked a lot like a buckwheat or a *Stephanomeria* whose common name was wire lettuce. I couldn't identify the plant for certain, but when I returned home I e-mailed photos to a Lancaster cooperative extension agent who was doing research with buckwheats, who told me that it looked to him like California buckwheat's winter appearance. Cool, I thought, two native California plants staking their claim in an abandoned (I hoped) field. What a combination for a garden! This wasn't just a little patch of poppies and a California buckwheat (*Eriogonum fasciculatum* var. *foliolosum*), it was a big-ass field of the stuff making a big flat grid of orange and red so strange that it suggested

Two golden-state plants—California poppy and California buckwheat—team up in an abandoned field.

an extraterrestrial landscape. I made a mental note for the next wildflower garden I would design: orange and burgundy make an unexpected but awfully nice color combination, especially when laid out like this in a wild checkerboard fashion.

All of the online wildflower chat says to photograph poppies midday, when they are wide open to the sun. To me this seemed like a recipe for overexposure except on a somewhat overcast day. Besides, the dense clouds hanging over Antelope Valley persisted, and I was out under a big gray sky—I didn't have a full-sun option. The poppy petals were chastely folded in cone shapes, and in the overcast light their orange was deep, saturated, and powerful. With their petals closed up, the poppies appeared both shy and defiant, but I enjoyed seeing them with the hatches battened down; the effect was more subtle, and the orange teardrop shapes of the flower heads added to their beauty.

The landscape alternated between orange poppies, yellow goldfields, and occasional hummocks of Joshua trees and rabbitbrush. The wind had picked up, and for the second day in a row I was getting wet. My mind drifted to thoughts of pork-and-bean *pupusas* in a warm booth at Teclena Flores, but first, I wanted a few more photos. In between squalls, I gripped the aluminum stanchions of my tripod and did my best to capture John Muir's great rich furred valley. If I squinted, it did indeed appear like a lake of sunshine, albeit a choppy pond on a windy day. Staring at the innumerable electric-carrot-colored poppy buds, I remembered that the Russian painter, Wassily Kandinsky, had written, "Orange is like a man, convinced of his own powers." I took a deep breath, hoping to inhale a large dose of poppy confidence before heading home.

Plants to find

California buckwheat *(Eriogonum fasciculatum var. foliolosum)*
California poppy *(Eschscholtzia californica)*
chia *(Salvia columbariae)*
Cooper's goldenbush *(Ericameria cooperi)*
fiddleneck *(Amsincaia sp.)*
goldfields *(Lasthenia californica)*
Joshua tree *(Yucca brevifolia)*
rabbitbrush or chamisa *(Ericameria nauseosa)*
thistle sage *(Salvia carduacea)*

Breakfast and wildflower info

Wee Vill Market
18348 West Avenue D
Lancaster, California
661-724-3001

Where to stay

The chains are your only options here, so choose something on the far north side of town toward the Antelope Valley California Poppy Reserve. Off Highway 14 near exit 44 you'll find an Oxford Inn and Suites as well as the budget Motel 6.

Where to eat

Teclena Flores
814 West Lancaster Boulevard
Lancaster, California
661-951-8590

What to read

Joshua Tree: Desolation Tango, by Deanne Stillman. University of Arizona Press, 2006.
Mojave Desert Wildflowers: A Field Guide to Wildflowers, Trees, and Shrubs of the Mojave Desert, by Pam MacKay. Falcon, 2003.

Bluebonnets, Barton Springs, Lady Bird, and Barbecue: Texas

When: *late April 2006*

Destination: *Austin, Texas*

Total trip time: *7 days*

Vehicle: *1999 VW Jetta TDI*

Roundtrip distance from Tucson: *about 2,000 miles*

My guide: *Colleen Belk of Barton Springs Nursery in Austin*

Music: Gone to Texas *(a mix I put together myself);* David Mead's Indiana

I DROVE OUT OF TUCSON TOWARD TEXAS with a head full of misconceptions about the Lone Star State. My idea of Texas-style living was something along the lines of a pickup truck, a manufactured home, five dogs, and a chain-link fence. A friend had compared the social climate in Texas to that of a high school full of grownups who were still in their respective jock and cheerleading cliques, and warned against entering the state in a foreign-made passenger car without a "W" bumper sticker. I expected a state full of aging cheerleaders and beer-drinking good ol' boys, similar to those depicted on the Fox animated series *King of the Hill*.

The author enjoying tacos at a roadside stand near Lordsburg, New Mexico.

My original purpose for venturing into the republic of Texas was presidential in nature. I aimed to photograph both the Lady Bird Johnson Wildflower Center and Laura Bush's garden. Getting into the Wildflower Center was no problem; Laura Bush's garden would prove otherwise. Some might wonder why I would be so curious about the first lady's garden, but I had my reasons. It had been featured by Ketzel Levine on an NPR gardening segment that I tuned into the middle of. I heard a female voice describing her garden in terms that would make environmentally conscious gardeners break into wide smiles. She talked about the need to conserve water (her own garden has a rainwater-harvesting cistern), the importance of native plants and how she likes to shop at the native-plant nurseries in Austin, and of all things, how we need to manage cattle responsibly to preserve our native flora! To my great surprise, this voice belonged to none other than Laura Bush.

My mental picture of the president's ranch in Crawford was 1,600 acres of brush and trouble. I had seen news footage of W out dimly "clearing brush" at the ranch, which he said was his favorite activity. This gave me a minor feeling of kinship with the commander-in-chief. I am much more at ease thinking of our president out hacking away at a mesquite thicket than sitting in a meeting with Dick Cheney talking about the legal definition of torture. Having W consider questions like "Can we dress them up in woman's clothes?" and "What about the dogs?" does not sit well. But picturing W out on the ranch in a cowboy hat, wielding a chainsaw, seemed to suit him. In fact, my own dim nature has at times led me to go out and hack down some brush for an afternoon or two, too.

In order to receive an invitation to the first lady's Crawford garden, I called my only good Republican insider friend, Mike Mower, deputy chief of staff for Jon M. Huntsman, the governor of Utah. Mike and I had worked together as Mormon missionaries in Oregon. We had been roommates with diametrically different political opinions. During the time we lived together, his wall was covered with *Time* and *Newsweek* covers of President Reagan (after one heated political discussion, I decorated each of the Reagan portraits with a mustache). Remarkably, we remained friends, and now Mike was open to pulling some strings for me. There was a high, nearly satanic, cost for Mike's help, if he got me access: I would

have to let him register me as a Republican. Hot after the first lady's garden, I figured that this would be the best motivation I could imagine for Mike, akin to holding a nice porterhouse steak under the nose of a bloodhound. Mike began making phone calls for me. I knew he was pulling all the strings he could. We changed tactics and asked if I could meet Laura Bush's gardener or landscape designer, hoping I could get into the garden through the service gate. He cc'd me on e-mails. Mike even wrote a letter on official Beehive State stationery to the director of the Office of Intergovernmental Affairs (not what it sounds like), in which he surprisingly described me as "talented" and "delightful."

To both of our great disappointment, we could not get anywhere near the presidential residence in Crawford. Our requests coincided with the nadir of Bush's popularity, and even though Mike's letters mentioned my skills as an author (questionable in my opinion, but Mike *is* a PR guy) and my admiration of the First Lady's garden ethics, our bid was doomed to failure. The White House was in trouble, and they were closing ranks and circling the wagons. Letting a little-known and fairly liberal garden writer onto the property was probably viewed as riskier than it was worth. "Think about your legacy!" I wanted to admonish, but I had no one to appeal to. Mike Mower later admitted that our requests were sent right in the middle of a rough patch between the White House and the state of Utah; the normally chummy relationship had suddenly turned chilly because the state of Utah was publicly threatening to opt out of Bush's "No Child Left Behind" program.

I was armed with guidebooks for travel into Texas. *Wildflowers of the Chihuahuan Desert* and

Legends of Texas Barbecue Cookbook both proved essential. In addition, I had a ten-CD set of Matt Dillon reading Jack Kerouac's *On the Road*, which would help eat up the big miles between me and Austin. When I got weary of Kerouac, the soundtrack to my trip was a mix called *Gone to Texas*, which featured a bunch of Texas artists like Billy Joe Shaver, Guy Clark, Townes Van Zandt, Robert Earl Keen, Terry Allen, and the Austin Lounge Lizards. In his song "Gone to Texas," Terry Allen sums it up this way: "You say it ain't no different [than] any other place you go, well you must be a Yankee or you're just kind of slow."

The drive out of Arizona and across southern New Mexico was bone-dry, and I began to wonder if I would see wildflowers at all. Even the roadsides, which normally receive extra rainwater off the tarmac, were tawny with last year's dried flowers and grasses. I listened to David Mead's song "New Mexico" thinking about how much, even with this drought, I loved this state, so similar to my Arizona, yet different. New Mexico is like a cooler, less-affluent Arizona with a big river running right through its center. I love the plants, the geology, the people, and most of all the food. Even in the Southwest, "New Mexican" cuisine is strangely confined to the state, though food writer Calvin Trillin has long advocated for its export to Manhattan. The entire cuisine is based on a trio of New World produce—chile, corn, and beans. New Mexico red chiles taste like no others; their deep, sun-filled flavor is like sun-dried tomatoes and campfire smoke. I bought a bag of dried mild red chiles in Las Cruces and ate them like spicy jerky as I crossed the state.

As I passed through the Mesilla Valley, I looked up at the rugged Organ Mountains and thought about how many plant treasures nestled in the folds and creases of their rock faces. Just before I entered Texas at El Paso, yellow flashes of paper flower (*Psilostrophe cooperi*) appeared on the roadside; I smiled at the tenacious disposition of these scrappy plants. I stopped at the Chihuahuan Desert Gardens there and photographed a big red stand of cardinal penstemon (*Penstemon cardinalis*) and ate excellent red-chile enchiladas out of a Styrofoam container in the Barnes & Noble parking lot. There is nothing worse than eating alone, except eating alone while other people are watching you eat alone. I prefer the solitude of my Jetta cockpit, even if it means later vacuuming out stray bits of wilted lettuce from between the seats.

Those who had warned me about the big boring stretches of west Texas hadn't been paying close enough attention to the roadsides. The big dome of the blue sky overhead, the dust, and the twisted and struggling mesquite trees combined to make this Arizonan feel quite comfortable, reminding me of the title of Gretel Ehrlich's book, *The Solace of Open Spaces*. Driving west to east was new to me. Glancing at the rugged, sawtooth-profiled mountains east of El Paso gave me geologic comfort. Rather than experiencing a monotonous haul, I found myself stopping to admire purple prickly pear (*Opuntia gossaliniana*) and sundrops (*Calylophus hartwegii*) beside the road. The purple prickly pear I found on some grazing land beside the road had wonderful long mahogany-colored spines. I picked up a cow-chewed cactus pad and noticed *Calylophus* growing beside the road, along with a handsome little plant with a black stigma and corolla that looked a little like a bumblebee.

The flats of west Texas were filled with my peeps. Ocotillo, soap tree yucca (*Yucca elata*), prickly pear, and agave. I even got to see a small evening primrose (*Oenothera* sp.) growing in a perfect round mound in the freeway median. Its little white flowers glowed as semis blew by me on the freeway; I caught them in the early glowing light while the flowers were still open wide.

After traveling across the long stretches of west Texas, I came to the town of Sonora, and all of a sudden, I was in oak country. I thought about my friend David Cristiani and how much he would enjoy seeing these heat-tolerant oaks with me; David loves oaks so much that he named his New Mexico landscape-design company after their genus name, *Quercus*. I had begun to climb up onto the vast limestone plateau country surrounding Austin. As I turned onto Highway 290, I was finally off the concrete ribbon of I-10 and into the rolling hills of the legendary Texas Hill Country. Before I got to Fredericksburg, I had pulled over several times for first sightings of plants. Thriving along Highway 290, I saw Texas violet sage (*Salvia farinacea*); evening rain lilies (*Cooperia drummondii*); firewheel (*Gaillardia pulchella,* also called blanketflower); winecups (*Callirhoe involucrata*); and the ubiquitous (in Arizona) garden plant, Mexican evening primrose (*Oenothera speciosa* or *Oenothera berlandieri*). All of these were wonderful wild relatives to plants that were becoming common in domesticated desert gardens. I took advantage of the wide, green road shoulders to take pictures.

Since I was smack in the middle of Texas's German belt, I stopped for lunch in Fredericksburg at the Auslander Biergarten, which just called out to me from amidst the quaint but

Firewheel.

touristy storefronts. Not only did this place have lots of local and imported beer (I ordered a Shiner Blonde), and a dish called "Texaschnitzel," the floor of the whole restaurant, inside and out, was gravel—a garden touch that I thought was just splendid. To top things off, a blackboard above the bar announced that Joe Ely and Billy Joe Shaver, two of the very artists on my *Gone to Texas* mix, were coming to the Auslander later in the summer. The Auslander was my first taste of the kind of friendly, tolerant Texas culture that I would encounter everywhere in Austin.

As I climbed up to Austin, I began noticing huge twisted mounds of yucca growing under oaks and mesquites, which I thought had to be twisted-leaf yucca (*Yucca rupicola*). This plant is relatively rare in the Arizona nursery trade and commands a high price at local nurseries, and here it was everywhere, like a big roadside weed. This was a plant that could find a great home beneath the

Mexican blue oaks (*Quercus oblongifolia*), escarpment live oaks (*Quercus fusiliformis*), or even regular old scrub oaks (*Quercus turbinella*), in Tucson, Sonoita, and Patagonia; for even more garden-design fun, you could plant a wild circle of rain lilies (*Zephranthes candida*) around the twisted-leaf yuccas.

Through a mutual friend, I had the great pleasure of staying with a fine Austin gardener and plantswoman, Colleen Belk, who would prove to be an invaluable guide to the Austin garden scene. Colleen manages Barton Springs Nursery, considered one of the best native-plant nurseries in the region—so good, in fact, that Laura Bush *does* occasionally shop there. As it worked out, Barton Springs Nursery was about as close as I would get to the First Lady. When I first talked to Colleen on the phone and mentioned that I was going to try to see the First Lady's garden, Colleen said, "You know he's not real popular around here right now." Her enthusiasm and general Texas friendliness were contagious, and I liked her right away. Contrary to my fears, the most popular bumper sticker in Austin was not "W" or "Viva Bush" or even "Support Our Troops," but rather "Keep Austin Weird."

Colleen and her husband, Brad, had built a fun little vernacular corrugated-steel house, nestled in the oak trees in the hills near Lake Austin. The crowning architectural feature of the house was a truly giant covered back deck, complete with hammocks, outdoor dining, and a fire pit. Colleen was warm and friendly, and we spent the whole first evening looking at her extensive garden. She was a hands-on gardener whose plant collection included specialties from the likes of Mississippi's Felder Rushing. Colleen's can-do attitude reminded me that to make a garden in Arizona or Texas or New Mexico, you don't need a pedigree, you just need a shovel—well, okay, maybe a pick or jackhammer. Colleen had just dug in, built a home, made a career, had a family, and constructed a garden.

My first full day in Austin began with a trip to Barton Springs Nursery and a dip in the actual Barton Springs, which is the most magnificent natural pool I've ever swum in. The springs form a gorgeous clear limestone-lined pool near the center of Austin that stays an even 68 degrees year-round. Each day, 32 million gallons of water from the Edwards Aquifer bubble into Barton Springs. Refreshed from my swim, I poked around gardens with Colleen in Austin, finding some real gems, including the gardens outside the Hotel San José, which were new and edgy and fun. The planting strip in front of the hotel had a strange mix of Mexican feather grass (*Nassella tenuissima*, formerly *Stipa tenuissima*), century plant (*Agave americana*), and walls covered with creeping fig (*Ficus pumila*)—things I might not have grouped together, but things that seemed to work here. The garden was full of little outdoor rooms with chunky wooden furniture set on raked gravel. The gardens were designed by the team from Big Red Sun Nursery, where we stopped later in the afternoon. Next door to the San Carlos, we got coffee at Jo's, a cool outdoor coffee place attached to the hotel. At Jo's we enjoyed rubbing shoulders with Austin's young hipsters under a canvas awning on Congress Avenue.

Everywhere I went in Texas, people told me this was the worst year for wildflowers that they could remember. What they really meant was that the spring of 2006 was the worst year for Texas bluebonnets (*Lupinus texensis*). It seems that in central Texas, bluebonnets and wildflowers are synonymous. As I mentioned earlier, I had seen lots of roadside flowers in the Hill Country, but the vast fields of bluebonnets were not out there—too little rain, too late in the season. Based on what I had seen beside the road, I got up early and went out to Lady Bird to see just how bad it was.

The Lady Bird Johnson Wildflower Center is an exquisite collection of stone buildings, towers, and rainwater-harvesting tanks set in the middle of a vast woods and grasses, and in a good year, lots of wildflowers. Lady Bird did not just have the wild-flower center named after her; she built the damn place and supervised its design. Lady Bird is at least as crazy about desert flowers as I am, and when reading about her, I couldn't help but feel a kinship. The buildings, including a stone tower, provide places to take in the big views. On my visit, I was barely out of the car when I began photographing the evening rain lilies growing up next to prickly pear cactus. The combination delighted me, and the more I looked, the more lilies and prickly pear I found.

On my way to the offices of the Wildflower Center, I ran into Dr. Damon Waitt, the center's senior botanist, who again told me, "This is the worst wildflower year in thirty years." I mentioned that, compared to Arizona, it didn't look half bad. With that, Dr. Wait told me to look in the grasses for a special milkweed called antelope horns (*Asclepias asperula* ssp. *capricornu*). With his encouragement, I was out on the Meadows Trail right away and soon standing over the plant, which in my estimation was having a pretty good bloom year! Its flower was a hemisphere of cream and burgundy that reminded me of nineteenth-century jewelry—a lovely plant all the way

around. In the same meadow as the milkweed, a good display of firewheel was at or near its peak. I also spied a grass that appeared to sprout ganglia of tiny pink pipe cleaners from its seed head—both strange and lovely.

In the more formal gardens at Lady Bird, I found nice displays of winecups with square-bud primrose (*Calylophus berlandieri*); I also found angelita daisy (*Tetraneuris acualis*) going great guns next to more evening rain lilies and pale-leaf yucca (*Yucca pallida*). I also glimpsed the big silvery leaves of the Missouri evening primrose (*Oenothera macrocarpa*, also called *O. missourensis*) mingling with yet more winecups. In the central courtyard, I found the beloved Texas bluebonnets planted next to some café tables. So, maybe I was cheating just a little by calling these nurtured blue jewels "wildflowers," but I had come clear to Texas and couldn't leave without saying that I had seen some bluebonnets. Texans are manic for their bluebonnets to the extent that they have even adopted a state song celebrating the flowers:

Texas bluebonnets (Lupinus texensis) *at the Lady Bird Johnson Wildflower Center.*

Bluebonnets, so gorgeous and stately,
In your mantle of blue and of green,
In the spring when you're in your full glory,
You're the loveliest sight ever seen.

I'm a sucker for this kind of wildflower worship and think our country would be better off if we all praised flowers a little more. I don't even care if there are a few little inaccuracies, as in Nanci Griffith's "Gulf Coast Highway," in which she sings, "this is the only place on earth bluebonnets grow and once a year they come and go at this old house here by the road." Although many varieties of bluebells (lupines) bloom all over the West, I can understand the desire to believe that your wildflowers *only* belong to your home dirt.

Texans love their bluebonnets so much that they even plasticize them. Author Susan Lowell told me that after she read to some El Paso school kids, they gave her some plastic sprays of bluebonnets, along with a packet of genuine "Texas Dirt" as thank-you gifts and mementos. When you get to the point of plasticizing your flowers, that's some serious state-flower idol worship.

I stayed at the wildflower center until late afternoon, and by then I had worked up a mighty appetite. I drove on down to Lockhart to eat at Smitty's Market. The walls at Smitty's are black from years—decades really—of smoke "varnish." You open a screen door and walk down a long hallway toward an open fire on the floor near an L-shaped brick rectangle (these are the smokers) with a chopping block in the middle. The whole setup looks downright dangerous, and I hoped that no lawyers would ever try to get them to change it, because food cooked this primitively is profoundly comforting. I ordered two pounds of

brisket, which was hauled out of the depths of the smoker and cut up for me and wrapped in butcher paper. My mouth was watering as I sat down to eat. In Smitty's old dining halls, the knives are chained to the tables, I suppose to prevent theft, fights, or both. The new hall is bright and regular, but the meat is still something to fight over. The brisket was perfect, juicy, with a crunchy outer rind and a sweet post-oak flavor throughout. This kind of eating made me briefly consider abandoning all of my gardening and wildflower chasing to devote myself completely to barbecue.

I still had a couple of spots to check for wildflowers and one important sausage market to visit before leaving Texas. The next morning I drove east on Highway 290 toward the town of Elgin, officially recognized by the Texas state legislature as the "Sausage Capitol of Texas." My middle name is Elgin, as is my father's, and I thought that it would be nearly criminal not to stop in at the Southside Market there in Elgin and get my father some namesake "Elgin hot guts," a spicy, natural-casing, all-beef sausage, for his birthday. The operation at Southside has been a family business since 1882, and they produce enough sausage, as is depicted on their logo, to go link-to-link around the perimeter of Texas. I picked up a package for my dad but couldn't resist a lunch platter of hot guts for Elgin the younger. It was so good, so smoky and rich, the kind of meal where you say to yourself, "Heart, arteries, brace yourselves."

While in a convenience store in Elgin buying a bag of ice to cool my dad's hot guts, I overheard the very overweight clerk talking to a young man wearing a Sears polo shirt. The clerk said, "How d'ya like it over there?" motioning with his head to the new Sears store across the highway and without waiting for the Sears shirt to respond, "I was gonna work there but they were gonna make me tuck my shirt in and I couldn't do it."

"Hmmm," I thought to myself, "this is just precisely the kind of dilemma that living in the Sausage Capitol of Texas can get you into."

On some hilly back roads south of Brenham, I ran into a lovely display of clasping coneflower (*Dracopis amplexicaulis*), a plant whose yellow and red daisies resemble both Mexican hat (*Ratibida columnaris*, also called coneflower) and black-eyed Susan (*Rudbeckia hirta*), but are neither. In fact the plant is its own monotypic genus, meaning it is the only plant in its genus group. It was unbelievably dense. In my two years of chasing wildflowers around the West, this roadside patch was the most filled in, the most full-blown, the most lush and colorful flowers, I had yet encountered. This was also the furthest point east I had journeyed and likely the wettest spot as well. I looked on the map and realized that I was nearly to Houston, which receives almost fifty inches of rain a year! This is opposed to thirty in Austin and eight in El Paso. It occurred to me that I had strayed out of my target range for this book—I had chased wildflowers clear into the southeastern U.S. I decided that it was time to get the hell out of the East. I took the back roads south through Bellville and Cat Springs, stopping at an old gas station with "Cat Springs Country Club" painted over the entry, to get a cold bottled Coca-Cola and ask directions.

The Cat Springs Country Club folks got me back on I-10 toward El Paso and eventually Tucson. I hightailed it west, stopping only twice— once to photograph a field of prickly poppies (*Argemone platyceras*) from a church parking lot,

A field of prickly poppy near Bellville, Texas.

and once for a taco in a thunderstorm outside Lordsburg. I was out of Texas without harm, with memories of wildflowers in the place where the West meets the South.

Plants to find

angelita daisy *(Tetraneuris acualis)*

antelope horns *(Asclepias asperula* ssp. *capricornu)*

cardinal penstemon *(Penstemon cardinalis)*

clasping coneflower *(Dracopis amplexicaulis)*

escarpment live oak *(Quercus fusiliformis)*

evening primrose *(Oenothera* sp.)

evening rain lilies *(Cooperia drummondii)*

firewheel or blanketflower *(Gaillardia pulchella)*

Mexican evening primrose *(Oenothera speciosa* or *Oenothera berlandieri)*

Missouri evening primrose *(Oenothera macrocarpa* or *Oenothera missourensis)*

pale-leaf yucca *(Yucca pallida)*

paper flower *(Psilostrophe cooperi)*

prickly poppy *(Argemone platyceras)*

purple prickly pear *(Opuntia gossaliniana)*

square-bud primrose *(Calylophus berlandieri)*

sundrops *(Calylophus hartwegii)*

Texas bluebonnets *(Lupinus texensis)*

Texas violet sage *(Salvia farinacea)*

twisted-leaf yucca *(Yucca rupicola)*

winecups *(Callirhoe involucrata)*

Where to stay

Hotel San José

An urban bungalow-style hotel that has risen from the ashes of the original San José, which was built in 1939 as an "ultramodern motor court." It might be the coolest place to stay in all of Austin.

1316 South Congress Avenue

Austin, Texas

800-574-8897, www.sanjosehotel.com

Where to eat

The Auslander Biergarten

The Auslander's Texaschnitzel is a local twist on an Old World favorite! Hand-breaded cutlet topped with ranchero sauce, Monterey Jack cheese, sour cream, and guacamole. Gotta try it!

323 East Main Street

Fredericksburg, Texas

830-997-7714, www.theauslander.com

Smitty's Market

208 South Commerce Street

Lockhart, Texas

512-398-9344

Southside Market and Barbeque

1212 Highway 290 West

Elgin, Texas

512-281-4650

www.southsidemarket.com

Where to swim

Barton Springs Pool

512-476-9044

2201 Barton Springs Road

Austin, Texas

Where to find plants (to look at and/or to buy)

Lady Bird Johnson Wildflower Center

4801 La Crosse Avenue

Austin, Texas

512-292-4100, www.wildflower.org

Barton Springs Nursery

3601 Bee Caves Road

Austin, Texas

512-328-6655

Big Red Sun Nursery

1102 East Cesar Chavez

Austin, Texas

512-480-0688, www.bigredsun.com

What to read

The Legend of the Bluebonnet: An Old Tale of Texas, by Tomie de Paola. Putnam, 1983.

Legends of Texas Barbecue Cookbook: Recipes and Recollections from the Pit Bosses, by Robb Walsh. Chronicle Books, 2002.

Northern Chihuahuan Desert Wildflowers, by Steve West. Falcon, 2000.

Primrose by Tram: Snowbird, Utah

When: *Late July 2006*
Destination: *Little Cottonwood Canyon, near Salt Lake City*
Total trip time: *3 days*
Vehicle: *1999 VW Jetta TDI*
Roundtrip distance from Tucson: *1,600 miles*
Traveling companions: *a small army of NARGS plant-heads*
Music: *Josh Rouse's* Nashville

THE AERIAL TRAM AT SNOWBIRD whisks you to the top of Hidden Peak, at a heady elevation of 11,000 feet above sea level, and spits you out on a platform above a treeless pile of rocks. For someone who just flew in from Delaware or Seattle, the two-mile-high elevation can be *literally* breathtaking. Even for a desert rat arriving from the relative highlands of Tucson (approximately 2,600 feet), the air felt suspiciously thin, cool, and dust-free.

I came to Snowbird Resort above Salt Lake to participate in the North American Rock Garden Society's interim conference. Enticed by the copy on the NARGS website, which asked, "Tired of sitting in dark lecture halls, just talking about the gorgeous flora of our Western mountains? Dying to get out there and see, smell, touch the real thing?" I decided that I couldn't miss this wildflower event just one arid state north. The six-day event would consist of two days of lectures and four days of fieldwork in different mountain ranges near Salt Lake City. Although I went to college in Salt Lake City and lived at the mouth of the next canyon south of Little Cottonwood (the canyon in which Snowbird sits), it was inappropriately unfamiliar to me. I had been successfully avoiding many of the aforementioned dark lecture halls since college, but I was interested in

American Fork Twin Peaks, languid lady, and silvery lupine.

finding some unusual wildflowers with a few other kindred spirits and wildflower wanderers.

The North American Rock Garden Society, or NARGS, as it is more commonly known, is where serious gardeners, explorers, and plant geeks meet. From the first night of the conference, I knew I was in the company of an elite group, and that just keeping up with my fellow botanizers would test my skills.

Immediately upon my arrival, I commenced with a program of altitude adjustment and total immersion in the NARGS subculture. Ensconced in the luxuries of the summer resort at Snowbird, I swam laps on the rooftop pool, boiled myself in the Jacuzzi, and downed a pint of porter in the tenth-floor Aerie bar to aid in the acclimatization process. Serendipitously, I ended up having a beer with Sean Hogan, an extraordinary plantsman whose Portland, Oregon, nursery, Cistus, was doing a booming trade in Southwestern specialties like yuccas and agaves. "Portland," Hogan explained, "is at the northwest edge of the Southwest," an assertion that seemed both dubious and true. I knew that Portland, unlike other parts of the Northwest, received only twenty-eight inches of annual rain, nearly all of which fell during the winter months. Just back from a plant-exploring trip to Mexico, Sean was rattling off a dazzling array of new species that he had collected and propagated, and I made a mental note to visit Cistus next time I was in Portland and meanwhile to check out their online catalog. Sean told me of two particular yuccas that got my attention. Sean had been growing a tiny blue species from Utah's San Rafael Swell that he described as appearing like "blue starfish playing leapfrog" (*Yucca nana*). Another small yucca from Sonora, *Yucca endlich-iana*, Sean described as having black-purple flowers and forming a bulbous caudex suitable for bonsai. I found out that Sean traveled on plant- and seed-collecting trips with noted explorers and botanists like Arizona's Richard Felger, Ron Gass, and Greg Starr. His passion for desert plants was obvious. Sitting at a table high up in the Aerie, looking out over the tops of subalpine fir and Engelmann's spruce, talking about desert plants with a fellow rosette-fancier seemed incongruous if not a little ridiculous, but it was awfully fun.

The first full day of the conference began in a dark lecture hall talking about the gorgeous flora of our Western mountains. A plant-head at heart, I took a certain voyeuristic pleasure in seeing slides of plants, but vicarious experience has its limits. Just outside our Cliff Lodge accommodations were alpine plants of world-class beauty, and sitting in a warm conference room after breakfast seemed more like the fast track to nodding off rather than education. After one particularly long session, I found Cathy King, a keen Salt Lake rock gardener and one of the conference's organizers, who encouraged me to take the aerial tram. I bought a tram ticket and got out of a conference room and up on the mountain.

I boarded the tram with a backpack full of take-out fish tacos and taquitos from El Chanate restaurant at Snowbird, two liters of water, and a bottle of Virgin Vines Shiraz from a Utah State Liquor Store. The wine's label, in a kind of "it's cool not to know about wine" Richard Branson marketing angle, stated, "Dare to enjoy this wine without dashes of pretentiousness or hints of snootiness. Virgin Vines believes wine should be all about having fun and loving the taste ... not waxing poetically about meaningless wine-speak

Snowbird aerial tram: the express route to Wasatch wildflower hunting.

and food pairings." Sir Richard's advice about avoiding snootiness seemed a little suspect for a billionaire's wine label, but I liked the general message; agonizing about a wine pairing was not the domain of a guy with a backpack full of fish tacos, cameras, and wildflower guidebooks on his way up to two miles above sea level. The hot Mexican food emitted pungent garlic and grease smells in the tram, which no doubt tantalized and/or disgusted my fellow tram riders. Looking down from the tram, I began to notice large stands of blue-flowered plants clinging to the steep slopes. The tram, a quiet glass box, ascended the mountain with an uncommon smoothness. Not that I was accustomed to riding on trams—I've never been a downhill skier, and all of my going-up-mountains experience has been on foot. It occurred to me that, when available, the tram is an elegant vehicle to use on a wildflower trip—especially when you are pressed for time or un-accustomed to hiking up steep trails at very high

elevations. The tram is an acceptable wildflower shortcut.

Stepping off the tram, I experienced the expansive feeling that one often gets in majestic Western landscapes. The big geology, the panoramic view, the general in-your-face nature of a serious mountain or desert vista inspires awe. I walked across a slender ridge. On my right hand, the steep talus slope canting into the Gad Valley, on my left the summer green of Mineral Basin. For all its alpine beauty, the scree and shale inclines felt every bit as desolate and harsh an environ-ment as the giant sand dunes in the Pinacate that I had roamed in the spring of 2005. Sheer rock, bright white snowfields, intense sun and intense cold, the weight of 300 inches of snow—these challenges seem as formidable as any of those found in a blast-furnace desert.

Hiking south and west from the tram, there is no way to avoid the imposing stark American Fork Twin Peaks, a jagged pair of triangles with aprons of loose rock and snow below them. On my way toward the peaks, I encountered steep rock slopes covered with fields of silvery lupine (*Lupinus argenteus*). I thought to myself, "What a spec-tacular and adaptable plant family." I had seen arroyo lupine blooming near sea level in Organ Pipe Cactus National Monument in February, and Texas bluebonnets flowering in Austin in April, and here was their sister blooming her heart out two miles above sea level in late July. Seeing snowfields this far into summer made me hopeful that global warming hadn't yet melted every last patch of snow in North America. I gingerly picked a route out into the lupine slope, nearly slipping several times. This was a rather unforgiv-ing mountain. A misplaced step on the slippery

Splitleaf Indian paintbrush and silvery lupine.

talus would cause you to roll like a keg of beer into the Gad Valley or worse. The sun was bright and high, and I hunched down among the bushy lupine, set up my tripod and camera, and sat tight.

As I waited for the softer, glowing light of evening, I glanced upslope across the meadow and spotted a fellow rock gardener sitting amidst the lupine, ditching a lecture, waiting with camera in hand for the alpenglow, just like me. The only other people on the mountain were two teenagers fooling around up on the terminal platform of a ski lift. Aside from the occasional teen giggle, the mountain was quiet. After a short time I got hungry and started in on the tacos and taquitos. I considered uncorking the Shiraz but thought better of drinking at this altitude—particularly when more hiking lay ahead. Water was a better idea. Finally, a big puffy cloud slid over the sun, providing just the sort of light I was waiting for, and I jumped up to shoot photos, taking care not to cartwheel down the draw. While I clicked photos of the lupine and mountains, a duo of marmots stealthily approached the remnants of my fish tacos. I lazily flung a few rocks in their general direction to keep them in check. Marmots—best described as overweight, high-elevation prairie dogs—are highly social rodents who whistle back and forth to each other, signaling the arrival of fresh fried foods in hikers' backpacks.

Among the lupine were weeping blue-green leaves and flower clusters of the aptly named languid lady (*Mertensia ciliata*). Languid lady, also known as mountain bluebell, is a calming plant for me. The blue cast of its foliage and flowers recalls a still, cold, alpine lake. Unlike most of my barbed, spiky, and otherwise well-armed desert plants, the gentle feminine appearance of languid lady was refreshing among so much masculine geology. In contrast to languid lady, the perky and upright flowers of a yellow-orange version of the splitleaf Indian paintbrush (*Castilleja rhexifolia*) glowed like fire in the evening light against the peaks of the Wasatch mountain range.

White Colorado columbine mingles with languid lady.

As I followed the trail around the north face of the American Fork Twin Peaks, just before crossing a large snowfield, I spotted hot-pink flowers that appeared to be growing out of spinach-like mounds of greenery. I picked my way down the slope, which partially gave way with each step, hoping to avoid a mini-avalanche of rock and skinny wildflower hunter. As I got closer to my plants, I saw that the flowers were borne above the stalk, almost like a penstemon. They also shared their hot pink color with my favorite snapdragon, Parry's penstemon. I consulted my field guides and decided for certain that I had come across Parry's primrose (*Primula parryi*), discovered by the very same nineteenth-century botanist, C. C. Parry, who had found my beloved Parry's penstemon! Known among his peers as the "conciliatory pilgrim of botany across emergent West-America," Parry discovered many other plants, including one of the most handsome agaves, which is also named after him.

In my former life as a nursery manager, I had acquired a healthy disdain for the sort of annual primroses sold as "color." These primroses reminded me of a prudish English matron who would only reveal a mere ruffle of her petticoats after tedious pampering. In my mind, the plants corresponded with the dictionary definition of their prefix, prim: "stiffly formal and proper." I regarded them as greedy plants that required constant water in the cool months, only to promptly wilt at the first hint of summer heat; needless to say, I didn't expect to fall in love with one of them on a mountain range this rugged and stark.

In *Hamlet*, Shakespeare warns against he who down the "primrose path of dalliance treads." It seemed that this jagged Wasatch mountainside and these primroses were not what the Bard had in mind, if the primrose path was supposed to mean a garden path. The only creatures I could imagine summoning enough courage to engage in dalliance on this slope would be a pair of very randy mountain goats or a marmot couple who just finished off some unfortunate hiker's fish tacos.

To take my photos, I was obligated to stretch out across the loose talus, both to keep my balance and to position the tripod at a height low enough to frame both my primrose and the snowfields around it. With my ears down by the loose rock, I could hear a trickle—beneath the rock, there was water. Although my Parry's primrose appeared to spring out of a field of loose rock, pure snowmelt was flowing below the surface, keeping the spinach-like leaves perky and upright. The pink flowers glowed in the evening light, and I couldn't help but think how lucky I was to see this brassy snowmelt flower in its full splendor on a summer evening high above the rest of the Western world. I could imagine C. C. Parry traveling through this land, just barely settled by the Mormons, high up in a Utah canyon and seeing this plant for the first time, and the thought made me smile.

I huffed and puffed back up the trail to board that last tram down the mountain at 8:30 p.m. I stepped onto the tram at sunset and never broke into my bottle of Shiraz; I was already in an altered mental state, floating in the Wasatch mountain light, high on gray rock and spires of pink flowers.

Within hiking distance of Snowbird sits the little mining-town-turned-ski-town of Alta. Just barely outside the town is Albion Basin, which my NARGS brochure said was "considered one of

Utah's premier wildflower amphitheaters." Until I visited the basin, the word "amphitheater" conjured images of an IMAX cinema more than it did a place to see wildflowers, but as a venue for panoramic entertainment, Albion Basin did not disappoint.

In lieu of a NARGS banquet dinner, I opted for an evening hike in Albion Basin up the Catherine Pass Trail. I wondered if my mother, a Utah native and former tomboy who shared her name with this trail, had ever ascended her namesake route? As soon as I started up the granite and boulder-strewn path, with wildflowers exploding from every crack and recess, I knew that this was a magic place—a series of jewel-box gardens linked together with rock. The colors, which began with yellow whorled buckwheat (*Eriogonum heracleoides*) and orange-colored wavy leaf Indian paintbrushes (*Castilleja applegatei*), soon shifted to white and purple and pink beside a mountain rivulet of clear snowmelt. I saw a flower whose shape was unmistakable, but whose color nearly fooled me: the spire-like plant that was aptly named skyrocket (*Gilia aggregata*) was a shocking peachy-pink here instead of its usual fiery red. Further along, a strong and distinctly minty scent circulated around me—the result of brushing against giant hyssop (*Agastache urticifolia*) and horsemint (*Monardella ordoratissima*). I was passed by a couple of mountain bikers, laboring heavily up the steep grade.

At the top of a small plateau, the rocks turned to striped chocolate colors, and I was reminded of some brown limestone rock that I had once collected from the site of a future subdivision outside Tucson. Many of the chocolate rocks here in Albion Basin were near-perfect rectangles, as if a stonemason had hewn them into oversized shoe-

A hot peach-colored skyrocket amidst granite boulders.

box shapes. Not only were the rocks nicely shaped, they were arranged in neat patterns that harbored minute alpine plants, like rock penstemon (*Penstemon humilis*) and cushion phlox (*Phlox pulvinata*). At the base of these chocolate shoebox rocks was my favorite northern Utah flower, Wasatch penstemon (*Penstemon cyananthus*), whose iridescent blue and purple-tinged

Wasatch penstemon.

flowers are intense enough to break your heart. When I come to a wild place this intricate and beautiful, it usually makes me want to quit designing gardens altogether. How could such beauty ever be rivaled?

Strangely enough, these little wild vignettes get filed away in my head as benchmarks for the little back-yard gardens I draft in Tucson. Maybe I could evoke the *feeling* of Albion Basin. The arrangement of the chocolate shoebox rocks also reminded me of the similarities between classic Zen landscapes and Western gardens. My photographer friend Charles Mann writes that good Zen gardens share aesthetic elements with the best emerging dry-gardens of the southwestern U.S. Both, he argues, put an "emphasis on the forms of nature—rocks, shrubs, trees, dry water features, and understated structures." Charles goes on to say, and this is my favorite part, that "just like the desert in spring, occasionally [in Japanese gardens] there is a sudden dramatic surprise. When a particular fruit tree or shrub bursts into bloom, the effect can be startling..." That is what I want in the gardens I design: surprise! For a couple of months each spring, I want to startle my clients with wildflowers!

Other plant combinations of note included the lovely silver sage (*Artemisia cana*) combined with pink-flowered splitleaf Indian paintbrush (a pink version of *Castilleja rhexifolia*). As I climbed a high saddle, I passed a pretty young woman sitting on a rock writing in a journal; in a meadow beyond her, more lupine was blooming with lovely pale-pink sticky geraniums (*Geranium viscosissimum*), creating a pink and blue Victorian palette. The scene reminded me how fantastic life on Earth is, how much beauty is out there for us to

Variations on a theme: splitleaf Indian paintbrush.

discover. Seeing the wildflowers of the Albion Basin will erase a whole jumble of cell-phone ring-tones, junk e-mail, car payments, and credit-card bills from your cerebrum. It will fill your frontal lobes with the saturated color and dynamic geometry of wildflowers.

Plants to find in Snowbird

lanquid lady, mountain bluebells (*Mertensia ciliata*)

Parry's primrose (*Primula parryi*)

silvery lupine (*Lupinus argenteus*)

splitleaf Indian paintbrush (*Castilleja rhexifolia*)

white Colorado columbine (*Aquilegia caerulea* var. *albiflora*)

Plants to find in Snowbird Albion Basin

cushion phlox *(Phlox pulvinata)*

giant hyssop *(Agastache urticifolia)*

horsemint *(Monardella ordoratissima)*

mountain sunflower *(Helianthella uniflora)*

rock penstemon *(Penstemon humilis)*

silver sage *(Artemisia cana)*

skyrocket *(Gilia aggregata)*

splitleaf Indian paintbrush *(Castilleja rhexifolia)*

sticky geraniums *(Geranium viscosissimum)*

Wasatch penstemon *(Penstemon cyananthus)*

wavy leaf Indian paintbrush *(Castilleja applegatei)*

whorled buckwheat *(Eriogonum heracleoides)*

Where to stay

The Cliff Lodge at Snowbird

You can't beat the special summer rates (as little as $59 per night, depending on availability) and the mountain view from both pools alone is worth the price. Besides, you are just steps away from some of the best wildflower hunting in Utah.

Little Cottonwood Canyon, Utah

800-232-9542, www.snowbird.com

Where to eat

El Chanate

Unless you bring an ice chest with picnic provisions, you are restricted to the offerings at the resort. El Chanate's is probably your best choice for on-site eating at "the Bird," as the locals call it. The black-bean burritos are good, especially when ordered enchilada-style.

In the Cliff Lodge, Level A

801-933-2145, www.snowbird.com

....

One sticky geranium amid an army of mountain sunflowers (Helianthella uniflora).

Red Iguana

One good plan would be to haul up a take-out order of Red Iguana mole (I like the mole negro best, but all of the moles there are excellent) for a mountaintop picnic. Red Iguana may well serve the best mole north of the Mexican border. As an added bonus, the walls of the Red Iguana are autographed by members of the band Los Lobos, who stop in whenever they play Salt Lake City. If you plan to eat in the restaurant, be prepared for long waits; it is very popular.

736 West North Temple

Salt Lake City, Utah

801-322-1489, www.rediguana.com

Sawadee Thai

Exquisite and reasonably priced Thai in the heart of the city. The two dishes I sampled were aromatic and delectable and promised to temporarily erase the lingering effects or memories of altitude sickness: the Guay Teaw Pad Kee Mao (choice of chicken, beef, or pork) is fresh wide rice noodles and stir-fried meat with fresh Thai chile, garlic, mushroom, tomato, baby corn, and Thai basil in oyster sauce; the Thai Massaman Curry (choice of chicken, beef, or pork) has coconut milk, potatoes, carrots, and roasted peanuts.

754 East South Temple Street

Salt Lake City, Utah

801-EAT-THAI (801-328-8424), www.thaisiam.us

What to read

Great Basin Wildflowers: A Guide to Common Wildflowers of the High Deserts of Nevada, Utah, and Oregon, by Laird R. Blackwell. Falcon, 2006.

Utah Wildflowers, by Richard J. Shaw. Utah State University Press, 1995.

The Littlest Snapdragon in the World: Cedar Breaks, Utah

When: *late July 2006*

Destination: *Cedar Breaks and Red Rock Canyon, Utah*

Total trip time: *4 days*

Vehicle: *Lewis Brothers Stages Motor Coach*

Roundtrip distance from Tucson: *1,300 miles*

Traveling companions: *a small contingent of NARGS diehards*

Music: *Matthew Sweet and Susanna Hoffs,* Under the Covers, *Vol. 1*

AFTER ACCLIMATING to the high-elevation hiking at Snowbird, the NARGS group broke into individual expedition groups. On a roasting 100-degree day, we boarded a rather under-powered and worse-for-wear coach and drove south on I-15 with marginal air conditioning.

Our group included a range of sophisticated plant nuts, including a tree philosopher from San Francisco; two highly literate and entertaining gentlemen from Red Lion, Pennsylvania; a real plant technician, also from Pennsylvania, who carried the massive hardbound *Utah Flora* with him on all our hikes, along with a GPS, magnifying

A summer thunderstorm in red-rock country.

glass, compass, and probably several other con-cealed gadgets; a passionate young rock-gardening couple from Michigan; a pair of rainwater-harvesting Aussies; an engaging garden-book edi-tor from Massachusetts; and a postal worker from Illinois who could do a convincing Cliff Clavin impression from *Cheers* without trying.

Approaching Nephi, as we gained elevation, the bus groaned and rattled several times—even-tually overheating and stalling out on the freeway. There is nothing that galvanizes a group better than hardship, and I could be wrong, but I sensed a wave of excitement on the bus as my NARGS mates considered the possibility of revised plans. The NARGS veterans had known bus trouble on a previous trip and began recounting their ordeal. After a little while, though, the driver managed to restart the bus and get our group to a truck stop while a replacement bus was delivered. We got a big booth inside the truck stop café, ordered drinks, and sat around talking and browsing the plant lists for Cedar Breaks. The tree philosopher and I somehow got onto the topic of the human taste for sugar. He remarked that it begins as babies with lactose from mother's milk. He held up his arms in a wide U, tilted back his head and opened his mouth as if to receive a giant sweet cosmic nipple. Just in time, our replacement bus arrived and we were back on the road to Cedar City.

After settling into our lodgings at the Crystal City Inn, we boarded the bus and left for Kolob Canyon to enjoy a picnic dinner and some hiking and botanizing. Kolob Canyon's massive red sandstone spires rose from deep green flanks of pine and juniper species. While we admired the view, eating a picnic of cheese and baguettes with red wine, I met a young New Yorker named Brendan. We got onto the subject of architecture, and I found out that, like me, he was a fan of the architect Moshe Safdie, who had recently designed a new public library in Salt Lake City. I also learned that he worked at the new Museum of Modern Art in Manhattan, which I considered the most beautiful and understated museum I had ever seen. It was an odd moment, standing out in the silence of big red rocks, far from civilization, talking about a New York museum. I was surprised at the enthusiasm that Brendan and my new friends from Pennsylvania expressed about our strange and arid Western flora. We hiked along a ridgetop trail, finding mountain mahogany (*Cercocarpus montanus*), sheep fescue (*Festuca ovina*), and some

spiny and lovely red barberry (*Berberis haematocarpa*). We also encountered a tidy and compact shrub that I first mistook for a dwarf cliff rose (*Cowania mexicana*); the plant turned out to be antelope bitterbrush (*Purshia tridentata*), which has deservedly made its way into the Colorado nursery trade. This far south at this elevation, we had missed the main wildflower bloom by a couple of months, but there were still lots of interesting plants to inspect, and in the evening light the geology of the red rocks was inspiring on its own.

The next morning we headed to Cedar Breaks National Monument, which promised to have more in bloom by virtue of its higher elevation. As we boarded the bus, our Pennsylvanian plant technician passed out a revised plant list that he had downloaded off the Internet and re-sorted in Microsoft Excel for us. I was grateful for the re-sorting. I was still impressed and a little intimidated by the level of botanical expertise among my fellow travelers. I had a nurseryman's knowledge of plant taxonomy (the scientific naming of plants)—I knew the botanical names (genus, species) and common names of the plants in my part of the world, and, until this point, that had served me well. The first lists we were handed had the plant group, the plant family, and *then* the genus and species names. Yikes! I just wanted a list that was alphabetical by botanical name. While it was interesting to learn that my favorite genus, *Penstemon*, was in the Scrophulariaceae family, it was really more info than I needed, and it made it difficult to quickly scan the list for the plants I recognized.

Identifying plants through their botanical characteristics (and sometimes by the minutiae of their flower parts), often referred to as "keying a plant out," can be a tedious chore. I remembered that my own copy of *Arizona Flora* at home was often used to prop up my computer monitor. I did use it to find where certain plants were growing, but the keys were usually too ponderous. I preferred to learn the plants by having someone show me and explain the differences. As an example of how exacting a keying can be, in the key to the species for shrubby senna (*Senna wislizenii*), the description in *Arizona Flora* reads:

Stipules none [now what is a stipule again?]; leaflets caduceus [bulbous?]; fruits turgid, not more than 4 cm long. Plants shrubby [duh]; leaf rachis spinescent [huh?]; leaflets few and distant [wait, I thought the leaflets were caduceus?]; less than 1 cm long, thickish, oval or oblong-ovate; flowers in loose terminal panicles [whew...]

I'm not making light of the scholarship, fieldwork, and decades of heavy lifting that go into writing a definitive flora for a region (Thomas Kearney and Robert Peebles's *Arizona Flora* is over 1,000 pages and is printed in a small typeface), but I have to say that when I'm out on the trail, this level of botany is too cumbersome for my tastes. Give me a little regional Falcon guide with decent photos and a non-jargony description of the plant and where it is found. For my Cedar Breaks trip, I carried *Canyon Country Wildflowers* by Damian Fagan, which most of the time was up to the task.

From the top, Cedar Breaks is shaped like a large coliseum—a 2,000-foot-deep orange, red, and white bowl, with hoodoos, spires, and fins that poke out of the dish like eroded adobe architecture. There is nothing subtle about the geology of Cedar Breaks. This landscape could frighten anyone who is scared of heights or overwhelmed by panoramic views. An associate of mine from the wooded East described her first trip to the mountain West as an encounter with "violent" landscapes whose in-your-face boldness alarmed and frightened her. Cedar Breaks is just the kind of place to inspire this kind of fear. As I once heard Annie Dillard say, "We are uncomfortable admitting it, but violence can be beautiful." All in all, the geology of southern Utah has got to be some of the flashiest show-off geology anywhere. Sometimes, you walk along not noticing the plants because the rocks "talk" so loudly.

I slipped away from the group while an innocent young AmeriCorps volunteer delivered a junior-high-level geology lecture comparing the Cedar Breaks amphitheater to a layered birthday cake. The rock-savvy and prone-to-heckling NARGS group was barely able to endure the talk. Sneaking ahead, I took the Rampart Trial around the rim of the canyon while the morning light was still nice. I found scarlet paintbrush (*Castilleja miniata*) set against the orange canyon walls and a little meadow of pure blue western larkspur (*Delphinium* x *occidentale*) growing with yellow mountain sunflower helianthella (*Helianthella uniflora*) just off the trail. "Delphinium" is a loaded word, and a garden full of them implies the sort of sophisticated perennial garden found mostly on English estates or in moneyed Connecticut zip codes. A fellow garden writer and quick wit, my friend Paula Panich, begins a lecture about passion and obsession in garden writing by warning

....
Scarlet paintbrush perched on the rim at Cedar Breaks National Monument

that if "you think garden writing is about rattling teacups among the delphiniums, think again." These wild larkspurs wouldn't know the sound of a rattling teacup but are well adapted to the hazards of Western life.

The Rampart Trail ends on a narrow promontory dotted with ancient bristlecone pines (*Pinus longaeva*) that looked almost fossilized; they were weather-beaten and twisted and magnificent, with half of each plant resembling a dead snag and the other branches thick with needles. I had planted three bristlecone pines in my yard when I lived in Utah, and I always loved their deep-green, oversized pipe-cleaner-like branches—they were among my prized trees. As I approached the end of the trail, I spotted the plant technician sitting Indian-style with the substantial *Utah Flora* open on his lap. I had to admire his persistence, using the technical and somewhat obtuse *Flora* to key-out plants. On the other hand, here we were on this dramatic rock promenade above a world of orange, cream, and green, right next to ancient bristlecone pines, and he was *reading*? My motto was "shoot (photographs) first, and ask questions later," but even that, I realize, was putting the camera between me and the scenery—once removing me from the moment. I guess we all have our own way of making the landscape meaningful using the tools we are comfortable with—the camera for me, the *Flora* for the technician. Of course, this is probably why I'm a landscape designer and not a botanist; when faced with the Keatsian dilemma between truth and beauty, I choose beauty every time.

We spent the afternoon on the Alpine Pond Trail, which is also in Cedar Breaks, and its lovely namesake pond was a gorgeous oval with a circumference of Indian paintbrush. We returned to the Crystal Inn to relax in the pool under a sky of infinite Utah stars.

By the last morning of our excursion, I had become expert at the cooking of my own waffles in the buffet at the Crystal Inn. They provided the little Styrofoam cups of batter and the irons, and I stuffed myself each morning in preparation for our hikes. The waffles were chewy and sat in my stomach like wet shoe leather, which was a good thing for a skinny hiker with the metabolism

The ancient roots of this bristlecone pine cling to the edge of a canyon in Cedar Breaks National Monument.

of a rock squirrel. We pulled the bus onto a dirt road near Red Canyon and began walking down the road toward a series of red-rock mesas. Scrambling up the loose orange rock, I began to slide down, even in my grippy Merrill hiking boots. After changing my footing, I managed to make it up to a ridge. Looking downhill, I could see many of my fellow NARGS travelers were sliding backwards, and some had even resorted to a crablike ambulation to negotiate the slope. I gave those I could a hand up to the top.

Unfortunately, the first climb was not the last or the steepest ascent. We hiked across a backbone ridge, down through a saddle, and up one last steep loose pitch. I was third in a line of hikers when the woman in front of me, who against NARGS regulations was shod in tennis shoes rather than boots, began sliding butt-first toward me; I had to act fast to double-stiff-arm her derrière or risk rolling ass-over-teakettle down the red rocks with her. When we finally reached the top, the group sat under a tree and explored the flat rocks looking for some rare little cushion plant or another, which I believe was a vetch of some sort. I found it hard not to say, "*This* is the plant we came here for?" Everybody was really excited about this little thumbnail of a plant, and I chuckled to myself thinking about all of us, especially some of the less sure-footed baby boomers and seniors, risking their hides to see a plant no bigger than a half-dollar coin. Who says we lose our sense of adventure after thirty-nine?

What really excited *me* was on the lip of the mesa: some big granddaddy mahoganies. These were not the modest mountain mahoganies we had seen around Kolob Canyon, but rather the bigger, evergreen curl-leaf mountain mahogany

(*Cercocarpus ledifolius*), whose white trunks and deep green leaves spring out of pure rock. These particular plants were loaded with seed, which looks, well, like sperm with fuzzy tails. The seeds are designed to fall head-first, drilling their way into the soil with the tail acting like a kite's.

As we descended the mesa, two of my new friends from Red Lion, Morris and Nick, called out for me. Morris was red-faced with excitement, and I spotted his snowy white beard and close-cropped hair from some distance away. I had liked Morris right away; he was a New Mexico boy at heart. He loved red chile, mole, and Western geology, and he had even hung out with Edward Abbey. He knew that I had a thing for penstemons and exclaimed that he had to show me the smallest penstemon on earth. We hiked down the dusty dirt road to the approximate point where Morris remembered seeing it. "Shit!" he exclaimed, "it was right here!" We searched around for a few moments until Morris said, "Yes, here it is. I was beginning to think I

A most diminutive snapdragon (Painted Desert mat penstemon) and Morris's thumb and finger.

had lost my mind." Morris put his thumb beside a tiny silver mat with a single petite blue tubular flower. I set up my tripod at its lowest setting and photographed the plant with Morris's thumb next to it for scale; it was a variety of mat penstemon that Morris said was named after the Painted Desert. When I got home, I looked in my book and on the Internet for the name, but I could never verify the Painted Desert part. It didn't really matter; to me it will always be Morris's Painted Desert penstemon—the littlest penstemon on our blue marble. There I go choosing beauty again.

• •

Plants to find

antelope bitterbrush *(Purshia tridentata)*

bristlecone pines *(Pinus longaeva)*

cliff rose *(Cowania mexicana)*

curl-leaf mountain mahogany *(Cercocarpus ledifolius)*

mountain mahogany *(Cercocarpus montanus)*

mountain sunflower *(Helianthella uniflora)*

Painted Desert mat penstemon *(Penstemon caespitosus var. deserti pinta)*

red barberry *(Berberis haematocarpa)*

scarlet paintbrush *(Castilleja miniata)*

sheep fescue *(Festuca ovina)*

smoothleaf beardtongue *(Penstemon leiophyllos)*

sulphur buckwheat *(Eriogonum umbellatum)*

western larkspur *(Delphinium x occidentale)*

Where to stay

Crystal Inn

1575 West 200 North

Cedar City, Utah

435-586-8888

www.crystalinns.com/cdc.html

The blooms of this sulphur buckwheat hover over the plant like orange and yellow popcorn.

Where to eat

The Bard's Eating and Drinking Establishment (in the Crystal Inn)

Because the Utah Shakespeare Festival is in Cedar City, the Bard's is one of many local restaurants trying to hitch its wagon to an Elizabethan theme. Those restaurants that aren't overly timber-framed cottages are Western branding-iron-type steak and burger places. What can be said for the Bard's is that it is conveniently located in the motel and has a bar that serves the well-named Utah beers like Provo Girl.

1575 West 200 North
Cedar City, Utah
435-586-8888

What to see

Cedar Breaks National Monument
435-586-9451
www.nps.gov/cebr

Red Canyon
www.zionnational-park.com/red-canyon-utah.htm

What to read

The Anthropology of Turquoise: Reflections on Desert, Sea, Stone, and Sky, by Ellen Meloy. Vintage Books, 2003.

Canyon Country Wildflowers, by Damian Fagan. Falcon, 1998.

Rhapsody in Gentian Blue: Vail, Colorado

When: *late July 2006*
Destination: *the peaks around Vail, Colorado*
Total trip time: *3 days*
Vehicle: *1999 VW Jetta TDI*
Roundtrip distance from Tucson: *1,680 miles*
Traveling companions: *Lynn Hassler and Holly Lachowicz*
Music: *the New York Philharmonic performing Leonard Bernstein's "Three Dance Episodes"*
from On the Town; *George Gershwin's* Rhapsody in Blue; *Sergei Prokofiev's* Suite
from Cinderella; *and Maurice Ravel's* Boléro

I ARRIVED IN VAIL, COLORADO, as one of an elite group of vacationers who had slept in his car the previous night. My Jetta, caked in dust from the dirt roads of Utah's San Pete County, was looking distinctly down-market from the highly polished chrome-rimmed Cadillac Escalades and Range Rovers prowling the streets of the nation's celebrity ski town.

The previous night, I had made a beeline out of Salt Lake City toward the hinterlands of central Utah. I had planned to get a motel room in Spanish Fork, but the "no vacancy" signs glowed brightly, so I continued up the canyon until around 2:00 a.m., when I pulled into a state park and slept in the Jetta, beside the Spanish Fork

River. It was the kind of dark, clear desert night when the stars reveal themselves in incomprehensible numbers. Mine was the only car in the entire park campground, and I enjoyed the male pleasure of urinating outdoors in the cool night air. I had a partial box of French-Canadian chocolates called "Les Shooters" that contained dark chocolate cones filled with tequila, Grand Marnier, and other assorted liquors. I knew that if I didn't finish them off that night, they would surely melt as I traveled across the Utah desert toward Colorado the next day. These chocolates were no doubt contraband in San Pete County, which made me

Splitleaf Indian paintbrush (Castilleja rhexifolia)
near Shrine Ridge.

want to eat them to avoid a local asking, "What kind of chocolates you got there, son?" Even when eaten gluttonously in the rural Utah night, they *were* delicious. The chocolates, well, mainly their contents, served to make me comfortably numb to the difficulty of sleeping in a small passenger car, although I awoke bleary-eyed and in need of hydration the next morning.

I took an indirect route to Colorado, and one that involved searching for wildflowers. I turned south on Highway 89 toward Ephraim and Manti, following a tip about a penstemon bloom up Ephraim Canyon. As it turns out, I was a little late for the penstemon bloom and ended up driving twenty-three miles on a sketchy dirt road punctuated with rocks, deer, and elk, but few wildflowers. Looking for wildflowers risks going long distances for naught, and this was one of those mornings filled with weak Utah coffee and disappointment. Luckily, I was going to head uphill again, where my chances of finding wildflowers would be greatly enhanced.

At the invitation of my friend Lynn Hassler, a first-class birder and native-plant fanatic, I arrived at the Antlers at Vail, which featured a courtyard with a pair of large bronze bull elk butting heads in a bed full of annual flowers. Even to a Democrat without a vested interest in bronze garden sculpture, this was pretty impressive. Lynn was staying with her friend Holly Lachowicz, who had somehow procured our five-star lodging, which needless to say was not the norm for a wildflowering expedition. I slept on an overstuffed couch in a room with a large stone fireplace and Oriental carpets, while Holly and Lynn had their own rooms. I suppose the thought of a young married guy staying with two slightly older women in a posh Vail condo might seem strange to some people, but in the context of a wildflower hunt, it seemed perfectly natural and appropriate. Wildflower trips often involve travel to far-flung locales, and when you can find a comfortable (and free!) place to bunk with other wildflower enthusiasts, you don't get all Victorian about sleeping arrangements; it is a kind of underground railroad for wildflower hunters. Thankfully, Deirdre is not the jealous type anyway and was most likely happy to have my ceaseless plant banter temporarily directed at others. The whole condo, from the coffee to the maid service, was very comfortable indeed and a nice change from the rigors of camping and roughing it at the Motel 6. "I could get used to this," I thought to myself.

As a town, Vail can't help but ooze GOP. For heaven's sake, Gerald and Betty Ford are two of the town's most celebrated and revered residents—practically patron saints. The streets of Vail are quaint by design, and residents and tourists walk around with a moneyed and breezy ease that is infectious. I'm more accustomed to mountain towns like Flagstaff and Bisbee, Arizona, where hippies and artists walk around with dreadlocks, wearing cut-off jeans, and walking mixed-breed dogs on pieces of rope. Vail would take some getting used to.

On my first afternoon, I drove up to Vail Pass and hiked up Shrine Ridge. This was high subalpine terrain, and the road to the trailhead was the sort that could make the (second) aluminum oil pan on my Jetta a roadside curiosity. The one-lane dirt road had a tall center ridge peppered with embedded rocks. After slowly crisscrossing the hump a few times to protect my oil pan and dodge a roadside disaster, I parked under a tree and walked the rest of the road. The walk along the road was fortuitous. I came across a little meadow of elephant's head (*Pedicularis groenlandica*) covered with hairstreak butterflies. This deep-pink flower, as its name suggests, looks like a shaft covered with tiny, tusky little pink elephant heads. If flowers had political affiliations, I suppose this one would be a Republican. Whatever its leanings, elephant's head was a nice little flower previously unknown to me.

Looking out at the vista, the Colorado Rockies, although they are higher mountains than the Wasatch range, appeared more gentle and less violently geological than the sharp peaks of the Wasatch. I hiked up Shrine Ridge and stopped to admire a horizontal rock pile surrounded by scarlet paintbrush and a yellow daisy-like flower that I couldn't identify. Was it a sunflower, a mules ear, or a senecio of some sort? My field guides were of no real help here, and I was forced to relegate the little yellow daisies into the taxonomic purgatory that botanists call damn yellow composites, or DYCs. I climbed the little stone ridge and found that the tops of the rocks were covered with pockmarked depressions still full of rainwater. In the shallow soils between the rocks, sulphur buckwheat (*Eriogonum umbellatum*) grew, sending up its mini-cumulus-cloud-like flowers above the rocks. After dreamily looking out at the sunset, I realized that I was running out of time to get back to Vail and clean up for what promised to be a good Italian dinner. I packed up the camera and tripod and started trucking back down the mountain.

A shower and clean clothes greatly decreased my odds of getting picked up for vagrancy in Vail, and before I knew it, I was seated with friends around a warm table with a good bottle of Pinot Noir and a melt-in-your-mouth plate of gnocchi in front of me. Indeed, I felt a little like Tom Ripley, Matt Damon's character in *The Talented Mr. Ripley*. Not that I'm a pathological liar with a desire to brain a rich kid with an oar in order to assume his identity, but simply that I was circulating a few rungs up the ladder from my usual socio-economic *mise-en-scène*, and it was not at all unpleasant. How in the world had I ended up in this rather high-end Italian restaurant, Campo di Fiori, on a street filled with boutiques in which the lowest-priced item would likely be beyond my means, on a wildflower-

A tusky stand of elephant's head in a damp draw on Shrine Ridge.

Lynn Hassler and Holly Lachowicz enjoying
the flowers at the Vail Valley Music Festival.

hunting trip? Luckily, I was seated next to Lynn Hassler, who as a fellow plant-head and Tucsonan seemed a little starstruck herself. In fact, we gave each other a knowing smile during the appetizer of cherry tomatoes and buffalo mozzarella. Even Holly, who had been to Vail several times before on account of her brother-in-law's job organizing "Bravo! The Vail Valley Music Festival," appeared not altogether jaded. During dinner, we had a discussion about whether or not the Arkansas River actually flowed into Arkansas. Holly and Lynn had driven over the river the previous day. Lynn and I held that Arkansas was much too far east from Colorado for a river to make it there. We theorized that the Arkansas must flow into the Rio Grande somewhere. Holly disagreed, and

when we pulled my map out later that night, Holly was correct. For our geographical error, Lynn and I were ribbed at every stream and fork in the trail for the rest of the trip.

After dinner we walked down Meadow Drive admiring the blue Christmas lights strung up in Vail's street trees. After such a decadent dinner even a plant-hunting desert rat begins to feel a little like the local Izod-wearing après-ski royalty. Before bed we made plans for the next morning's trek, a route in the Holy Cross Wilderness to the Missouri Lakes at 11,500 feet that our guidebook described as full of "wildflower, lake and mountain landscapes worthy of calendar covers." Once our plans were set, I crashed on the sofa. Compared to my chocolate-liquor-induced car sleep, the couch at the Antlers felt cloudlike. I slept soundly and dreamt of subalpine meadows.

The trail up to the Missouri Lakes starts out gently enough, following a little stream under the canopy of trees, which made for shady hiking. Beneath the trees, bright red mushrooms grew, and near the stream we happened on a patch of gentians. For a person living in a desert—a place with a paucity of true blue flowers—seeing wild gentians was a real treat. The little fringed gentians (*Gentianopsis thermalis*) were growing in low-lying, damp little patches. The size of each flower and calyx (the base of the flower that holds the petals in place) were huge compared to the size of the little plants. The color of loyalty, of honesty, and truth was embodied in these little gentians. Looking at the fringed gentians reminded me that, amazingly, in a few hours we would be listening to the New York Philharmonic playing Gershwin's *Rhapsody in Blue* and Ravel's *Boléro*.

As we left the creek, the trail became steeper, heading up over the buttress roots of trees and chunky stair-step-like rocks. We soon discovered that the promise of calendar-cover landscapes was

The iconic state flower: Colorado columbine.

not hyperbole. The Missouri Creek that we were following became a charging torrent barreling down narrow rock chutes. Further along, the trail opened up into broad, wet meadows. The deep-purple western monk's hood (*Aconitum columbianum*) shot up in front of a stand of corn lily (*Veratrum californicum*). The sparse, ascetic architecture and hood-like structure lends an air of secrecy to this flower. Its flowers look as solemn as a bassoon. The top flap of the flower is closed so tightly over the sexual parts of the flower that it can only be pollinated by burly bumblebees strong enough to muscle under the hood.

One of our target flowers, a Colorado darling that is the state flower, Colorado columbine (*Aquilegia caerulea*), made its first showing below a rockslide near the trail. This flower, which is on highway signs, license plates, and Colorado memorabilia, is a sweet, innocent pale purple and white with cloverleaf-shaped leaves. Perhaps its most memorable features are the spurs that extend aero-

An *unidentified flaming red mushroom*.

dynamically from behind the petals. It is a hard plant to photograph on account of all the pale, almost white, petals. We rested for awhile in a wide meadow—the elevation was taking its toll. Holly had a little headache and vague nausea that caused us to pause until it passed. Then we pressed on.

We climbed up ridge after ridge, expecting to see the first of the Missouri Lakes at each crest. The mountains around us began to close in. We could see that we were nearing the tree line, and the rock faces of tall mountains became visible through the ever more spare trees around us. Three prominent peaks, all around 13,000 feet high, encircled us. When we reached the lake, we were ready to eat. We had packed prosciutto sandwiches, Trader Joe's dried apricots, apples, oranges, and nuts. At 11,500 feet, it was a feast, and I figured that in my two days in Vail, I had consumed more than my typical yearly allotment of prosciutto, but each bite was a treat. While we ate we looked around at the lake, which was still and surrounded by a mat of green punctuated by Whipple's penstemon (*Penstemon whippleanus*). On little rocky hillocks around the lake, I took photos of a little pale yellow paint-brush, which we surmised was *Castilleja rhexifolia* var. *sulphurea*, or sulphur paintbrush.

On account of threatening storm clouds and gravity, our descent was quick. We drove down the mountain to Vail, stopping back at the Antlers to wash up before the symphony. The pre-vious sentences only sound incongruous to those who don't have a summer house in Eagle County. Holly had an inside line on the concerts. The New York Philharmonic comes to Vail for around ten days each summer for a price tag of around

$1.4 million. My musical tastes run more toward power pop than symphonic pops, but this seemed like the best chance I was going to get to see—and more importantly, hear—what many call the best symphony orchestra on earth. We jumped on the bus and made it to the packed Gerald R. Ford Amphitheater just in time for three dance episodes from Leonard Bernstein's *On the Town*. We made our way to some comfortable boulder seats above the grass, which afforded us a great view of the Vail symphony set picnicking on the lawn. The smell of expensive cheese and corks hung over the lawn, and strawberries dipped in soft cheeses were placed in the mouths of babes; smoked salmon appeared from foil packages, and

LEFT: *The incredibly picturesque Missouri Creek.*
RIGHT: *The Missouri Lakes.*

intricately rolled sushi appeared from fancy wicker picnic baskets. All of this proved agonizingly appetizing for three famished hikers who had not left enough time for picnic preparations. We did enjoy flowers behind the rocks we were sitting on, and the captivating drum of Ravel's *Boléro* brought us back into the moment. I have no business commenting much on a symphony performance, other than to say that I liked it a lot—the perfect sonic bookend to a day in the wild. On the way home we walked through the excellent Betty Ford Alpine Gardens, which rightly brimmed full of native plants and boulders. I took pictures of the lovely nodding red-and-yellow western columbine (*Aquilegia formosa*) and admired the Colorado four o'clock (*Mirabilis multiflora*). The garden, situated so conveniently on the walk home from the symphony, was rugged and fun. What is it with these first ladies and their gardens? Is there some sort of contest I don't know about? If so, good luck beating Lady Bird—as nice as Betty

Western columbine.

Ford's gardens are, they barely hold a candle to Lady Bird's Wildflower Center.

After seeing and smelling the symphony crowd's gourmet picnic fixings, we were ready for dinner. We stopped for a sun-dried-tomato pizza, and Holly, a tequila connoisseur, bought us each a shot for good cheer on our walk home. We brought the pie home and consumed it while we downloaded the day's photos onto my laptop and broke out the field guides for positive identifications. Tomorrow, Lynn and Holly would leave the rarified air of Vail for the rarified air of Santa Fe; for me, the dusty pueblo of Tucson was calling my name.

I nearly got out of the Colorado high country without checking off one of the really important flowers on my list: Rocky Mountain penstemon (*Penstemon strictus*), but as I headed over to Denver on I-70, just before entering the Eisenhower/ Johnson Tunnel, I spotted some royal purple spikes along the road cut. I pulled over and ran across the freeway with my camera. Sure enough, Rocky Mountain penstemon in a loose, sandy slope so steep I could barely walk up it. I lay down on the sandy face, got my photos, got back in the car, and jetted east and then south, stopping twice to photograph soap tree yucca stalks in New Mexico—once near a line of derelict boxcars on an abandoned railroad siding and then against a thunderstorm sunset on the Continental Divide. The soap tree yucca is the state flower of New Mexico, and seeing its stiletto-like leaves and javelin stalks silhouetted against a technicolor sky seemed a fitting farewell to the Land of Enchantment. I crossed into Arizona and over the Dragoon Mountains in the moonlight, and by then I was almost home, ready to debrief my daughter, Zoë, about her first week of high school and reconnect with Deirdre.

Rocky Mountain penstemon on the I-70 road cut.

Plants to find

Colorado columbine *(Aquilegia caerulea)*

Colorado four o'clock *(Mirabilis multiflora)*

corn lily *(Veratrum californicum)*

elephant's head *(Pedicularis groenlandica)*

fringed gentians *(Gentianopsis thermalis)*

languid lady, mountain bluebells *(Mertensia ciliata)*

Parry's primrose *(Primula parryi)*

Rocky Mountain penstemon *(Penstemon strictus)*

scarlet paintbrush *(Castilleja miniata)*

soap tree yucca *(Yucca elata)*

splitleaf paintbrush (Castilleja rhexifolia)

sulphur buckwheat *(Eriogonum umbellatum)*

sulphur paintbrush *(Castilleja rhexifolia* var. *sulphurea)*

triangle-leaf senecio *(Senecio triangularis)*

western columbine *(Aquilegia formosa)*

western monk's hood *(Aconitum columbianum)*

Whipple's penstemon *(Penstemon whippleanus)*

Where to stay

Antlers at Vail

Luxury condos, close to everything, with bronze elk in the courtyard.

680 West Lionshead Place

Vail, Colorado

800-843-8245

www.antlersvail.com

Where to eat

Campo di Fiori

Excellent and not completely overpriced. For antipasti I suggest Ciliegine di Parma (cherry tomatoes, buffalo mozzarella, and Parma prosciutto with sun-dried tomato and basil pesto); for the main course, Gnocchi Trevisani (potato dumplings, red wine-braised radicchio and escarole, finished with smoked mozzarella).

100 East Meadow Drive

Vail, Colorado

970-476-8994

www.campodifiori.com

Pazzo's Pizzeria

This raucous joint is a good place to come if the rest of Vail gets too stuffy for you. Good pies are mostly under $20.

122 East Meadow Drive

Vail, Colorado

970-476-9026

Other botanical things to do

Betty Ford Alpine Gardens

183 Gore Creek Drive

Vail, Colorado

970-476-0103

www.bettyfordalpinegardens.org

What to read

Colorado's Best Wildflower Hikes, Vol. 2: The High Country, by Pamela Irwin, Westcliffe Publishers, 1999.

My Sweet Monsoon: Southeast Arizona Grassland

When: *August 15 and 22, 2006*
Destination: *Rosemont Junction and Patagonia, Arizona*
Total trip time: *6 hours*
Vehicle: *1999 VW Jetta TDI*
Roundtrip distance from Tucson: *40 miles*
Traveling companions: *Deirdre, my wife, and Zoë, our daughter*
Music: *Ryan Adams and the Cardinals,* Cold Roses

IT TURNED OUT THAT THE AWFUL parched spring of 2006 had a flip side: the glorious, cool, wet summer of 2006. To keep tabs on wildflower prospects, I'd become a bit of a weather junkie. While doing my daily surveillance of the National Weather Service's Tucson office website, I noticed that in June alone, our county received 135 percent of our normal June precipitation, and June's rain was just the beginning of the rain that started coming down that summer. The Pantano Wash and Rillito River, normally broad bone-dry washes, ran bank-to-bank in early August. Boulders the size of buses blocked the road and closed down

Twilight in San Raphael Valley, August 2006.

Sabino Canyon, one of southern Arizona's biggest tourist attractions. At my house my rain gauge had recorded nine inches from June 15 through August 15. I knew that out there in the desert, there were seeds in the damp shadows of rocks that couldn't help but germinate; a record bloom year for summer wildflowers was imminent. I got so excited that I had a hard time sleeping at night. For most of August, we slept with the windows open, and the cool, thick monsoon air and rat-a-tat sound of rainwater falling on our tin roof filled my head with visions of green mountains, running water, and hillsides covered with Arizona poppies.

Our monsoon season—subtropical thunderstorms that rumble out of the south and east from the northern states of Sonora and Chihuahua, Mexico, in July and August—is one of the sublime pleasures and secrets of desert living. While Philly and New York sweltered in sticky 100-degree-plus heat, we were enjoying the high eighties, with cooling afternoon rains. We hadn't experienced a seriously juicy monsoon season in a long time. I was more than ready for the wildflower mayhem that would surely follow.

I got my first taste of the great Sonoran Desert wildflower summer on a family picnic to the San Rafael Valley. On scenic Highway 83, the roadside was lush with *Mimosa dysocarpa* (velvet pod mimosa), a ferny little shrub covered with little fuzzy pink bloom spikes. We also passed clumps of yellow Mexican hat mixed in big expanses of

The star of the monsoon bloom: Arizona poppy.

firewheel, which had been hydroseeded (a wet mix of seeds and cellulose fiber often sprayed on roadcuts to prevent erosion and cultivate wild plants) along the roadside. Winding through the Empire Mountains toward the little town of Patagonia, the shoulders of the Patagonia Mountains were covered with Arizona poppies (*Kallstroemia grandiflora*), which glowed like military epaulets. I pulled over by a stretch of the old highway and hiked up a mesa to a meadow of Arizona poppy, startling a family of javelinas who lumbered up the steep hillside, knocking loose rocks downhill with their hooves in the process. Arizona poppies have a strange horticultural lineage in that they are related to the creosote bush. How is a little prostrate annual flower related to the hulking creosote? I love their orange petals, red-center eyes, and feathery leaves. I grew Arizona poppy in my garden, but after one good year of bloom it had nearly disappeared—I had read that it was a notoriously difficult plant to propagate and thrived best on total neglect (hmmm, now that does sound like creosote). Whatever conditions it needed to germinate, it had found them

Fuzzy velvet pod mimosa.

here on this rocky flat, where Arizona poppy flowed like a bright river.

Back at the car, we drove to the San Raphael Valley and watched the sunset over a pond surrounded by Mexican oaks. We ate turkey sandwiches by an old corral and headed back to Tucson under cover of darkness.

A week after our family trip to the San Raphael Valley, I couldn't get the southeastern Arizona grasslands out of my head. The rains continued, and I couldn't sleep. One mid-August morning, I woke at 4:00 a.m., got in the car, and drove to Rosemont Junction near Sonoita. Off Highway 83, I followed the winding dirt road past the signs warning that smugglers and illegal immigrants used this route. About four miles in, I stopped where the road crossed a dry wash, after glimpsing a flash of white on the right-hand side of the car—a steep rock hillside was covered with ocotillo and a small white-flowering plant. Leaving the car in the middle of the wash is a practice I can't recommend during the monsoon if you like finding your car where you left it, but I was lucky that day. As soon as I opened the car door, a strong jasmine-like scent hit me. I walked over to the rock face for a closer look and sure enough, these were white trumpets (*Telesiphonia brachysiphon*), a wonderful

Early-morning white trumpets.

Twining snapdragon.

little plant with dark-green leaves and a powerful perfume. My friend Greg had grown one in a pot outside his front door. From where they were grow-ing, I learned one thing for sure: they like fast-draining soil. This was a plant that should be in more desert gardens, but was almost never for sale. Just down the wash, I spotted an equally garden-worthy but seldom cultivated small vine: twining snapdragon (*Maurandya antirrhiniflora*). I had this plant in my garden, growing up an ocotillo fence, but I had never seen a handsome purple one like this in the desert. This rocky canyon was filled with vines. I saw two kinds of morning glory: scar-let creeper (*Ipomoea coccinea* var. *hederifolia*) and the more familiar canyon morning glory (*Ipomoea barbatisepala*). These should also be in many more Arizona gardens! The Arizona Department of Agriculture has what seems to me a misguided import ban on almost the entire genus Ipomoea, which includes even the above *native* species:

Scarlet creeper.

PROHIBITED: The following noxious weeds (includes plants, stolons, rhizomes, cuttings and seed) are prohibited from entry into the state:
Ipomoea spp. — Morning glory. All species except *Ipomoea carnea*, Mexican bush morning glory; *Ipomoea triloba*, three-lobed morning glory (which is considered a restricted pest); and *Ipomoea aborescens*, morning glory tree.

Sure, there are some nasty and aggressive *Ipomoeas*, including the dreaded bindweed, but these natives seemed no more dangerous than lots of other plants that are regularly sold at nurseries. Besides, these morning glories are heartbreakingly pretty! Come on aggies, get with the program— bring back the morning glories! "Hmm," I thought to myself, "I don't believe collecting seed from within the state constitutes a violation." Well, that was according to my reading…

Desert evening primrose near Rosemont Junction.

The Rosemont Junction area was spectacular. The plant variety was wide and bounteous. I found big yellow desert evening primrose (*Oenothera primiveris*). By the roadside a big hog of a plant, devil's claw (*Proboscidea parviflora*) was elbowing its way around the blue grama grass (*Bouteloua gracilis*). Here was the flower of the plant whose big gnarly seedpods we had hung in a chain from the rafters of our Bahía de los Angeles beach *palapa* back in March. Its flower, a white/pink/yellow number, was shaped a little like a penstemon flower on steroids. The flowers were provocative, with a yellow landing strip-like tongue leading pollinators back toward the business end of the flower. I was reminded of Ellen Malloy, who wrote, "flowers use color ruthlessly for sex."

In one species of devil's claw (*Proboscidea altheaefolia*, a yellow-flowering species), the pollen ripens before the flower opens. Industrious female bees cut round entry holes in the flower buds to get to the pollen. Unfortunately for the devil's claw, the species of bee, *Perdita hurdi*, once inside the cavernous floral tube, is too small to brush against the flower's sexual parts and adequately pollinate it. Enter the male *Perdita* bee. With more than nectar on his mind, the male will often kick back in the floral tube, waiting for a mate to appear. If things work out ("Hi, honey, how did a nice girl like you end up in a demonic flower like this? By the way, have I told you how much I like the black stripes on your tail? "), the resulting tango will smear a little pollen on the flower's stigma, leading to the wonderful green chile pepper-like fruit, and later, the dried curved black claws.

Beside a gravelly wash, I found two trumpet-shaped white flowers, one called paleflower skyrocket (*Ipomosis longiflora*) and another that I couldn't identify with bright pink stamens. I saw a crazy rainbow-striped cactus sitting in a bunch of Arizona poppies and figured it must be the Arizona rainbow hedgehog cactus (*Echinocereus rigidissimus*).

Before I drove back home out of Santa Cruz County, I turned down Highway 82 toward the town of Patagonia. When I was a boy, Patagonia was one of my favorite places. My father would take us to the Museum of the Horse, where they kept under glass the petrified corpse of a bandit who'd been caught in a sandstorm. Now, the museum is gone, but Patagonia still has its charms. I stopped outside of town to hike up the golden foothills of the Santa Rita Mountains. I had never seen Arizona poppies so thick. The hills glowed with orange. This bloom was better than the field of California poppies I had seen outside Lancaster. I ran up a ridge, scaring white-tailed deer from a thicket. The Arizona poppies grew from beneath stands of bear grass (*Nolina macrocarpa*) and desert spoon (*Dasylirion wheeleri*) and under Mexican blue oaks and velvet mesquite trees (*Prosopis juliflora*).

From the topmost foothills I could see the top of Mt. Wrightson. Looking around me in a big circle, the whole world looked orange. One of the pleasures of monsoon wildflower hunting is the solitude. There are very few flower peepers in the Sonoran Desert in August—all of the winter visitors are back in Cleveland, the traffic is light, the cafés are not crowded, and after a soaking monsoon like we had in 2006, the flowers are out in force. For my money, the flowers of late summer are as diverse and showy as our spring flowers. I loved being out on a cloudy morning in damp washes and on orange-blanketed hilltops. On my way back to the car, I found one last little flower, the lowly little crownpod purslane (*Portulaca umbraticola* var. *coronata*), whose red-and-yellow flower stared up at me like a tiny bloodshot eye. It was small but not at all unattractive—another plant that you couldn't buy if you wanted it. It gave me hope that I hadn't begun to exhaust the plant discoveries in the Southwest. There were plenty of frontiers and adventures for future plant-heads, and that was a very good feeling indeed.

● ●

Plants to find

Arizona poppy (*Kallstroemia grandiflora*)

Arizona rainbow hedgehog cactus (*Echinocereus rigidissimus*)

bear grass (*Nolina macrocarpa*)

blue grama grass (*Bouteloua gracilis*)

canyon morning glory (*Ipomoea barbatisepala*)

crownpod purslane (*Portulaca umbraticola* var. *coronata*)

desert evening primrose (*Oenothera primiveris*)

desert spoon (*Dasylirion wheeleri*)

devil's claw (*Proboscidea parviflora*)

firewheel or blanketflower (*Gaillardia pulchella*)

Mexican blue oak (*Quercus oblongifolia*)

Mexican hat or coneflower (*Ratibida columnaris*)

ocotillo (*Fouquieria splendens*)

paleflower skyrocket (*Ipomosis longiflora*)

scarlet creeper (*Ipomoea coccinea* var. *hederifolia*)

twining snapdragon (*Maurandya antirrhiniflora*)

velvet mesquite trees (*Prosopis juliflora*, formerly *Prosopis velutina*)

velvet pod mimosa (*Mimosa dysocarpa*)

white trumpets (*Telesiphonia brachysiphon*)

Where to stay

Spirit Tree Inn

Big cottonwood trees and stone fireplaces await you at this small B&B that is close to lots of birding and wildflower action.

3 Harshaw Creek Road

Patagonia, Arizona

520-401-0541 or 520-394-0121

www.spirittreeinn.com

Where to eat in Sonoita

The Grasslands Bakery & Café

The Grasslands is one of those rare mom-and-pop places that doesn't get its ingredients off a SYSCO truck. Really, how many restaurants can their own jellies, chutneys, and salsas? In addition to the canned items, the baked goods are wonderful. Throw some in your backpack or enjoy the patio.

3119 Highway 83

Sonoita, Arizona

520-455-4770

www.grasslandscafe.com

Velvet Elvis Pizza Company

If you don't smile at the name, this isn't the place for you. Try the following specialties, one of which requires a day's advance notice to prepare: The Exorcist (roasted red pepper, basil, gorgonzola and roasted garlic, mozzarella), and The Inca Quinoa Pizza (crust prepared with quinoa flour and baked in a deep iron skillet with layers of various vegetables and cheeses—requires 24 hours notice).

292 Naugle Avenue

Patagonia, Arizona

520-394-2102

www.velvetelvispizza.com

Where to eat in Tucson on your way to Sonoita

Los Pipos

Los Pipos is more of a hot-dog stand in the parking lot of Ace Hardware than a sit-down place, although café tables under a tent are available. Los Pipos serves up a norteño specialty: the Sonoran hot dog. The dog is wrapped in bacon, nestled in a fresh Mexican bakery bun, then covered with sautéed onions, beans, guacamole, mayo, and salsa. It is addictively yummy.

7451 South Houghton Road

520-663-5282

Tucson, Arizona

Javalina's Coffee

Great coffee at a locally owned place with free Internet and live local musical and literary entertainment.

9136 East Valencia

Tucson, Arizona

520-663-5282

www.javalinas.com

What to read

Sonoran Desert Wildflowers: A Field Guide to the Common Wildflowers of the Sonoran Desert, by Richard Spellenberg. Falcon, 2002.

Native Plants for Southwestern Landscapes, by Judy Mielke. University of Texas Press, 1993.

Wildflowers of the Desert Southwest, by Meg Quinn. Rio Nuevo Publishers, 2000.

Hummingbirds of the American West, by Lynn Hassler Kaufman. Rio Nuevo Publishers, 2001.

Huachuca: A Sky Island Butterfly Garden

When: *mid-September 2006*

Destination: *Garden Canyon, Huachuca Mountains*

Total trip time: *1 day*

Vehicle: *1998 Ford Explorer*

Roundtrip distance from Tucson: *124 miles*

Traveling companions: *Jim Brock and Lynn Hassler*

Music: *the fall breeze*

WE WERE NOT FAR down a dirt road headed up Garden Canyon when our driver, companion, and resident butterfly expert, Jim Brock—or "butt-head," as Lynn Hassler called him—exclaimed, "Look, I've got an Ares metalmark on my hood. I've never had an Ares metalmark on my hood." For Jim, this was not simple butterfly geekery; in the last twenty-six years, he had traveled up Garden Canyon over a hundred times looking for butterflies. He possesses intimate knowledge of the butterfly geography of Garden Canyon. On account of my long legs, I was riding shotgun, and Lynn was in the back seat. Lynn, a crack birder who is also on a first-name basis with the canyon, has a mental map of the location of nearly every exceptional Huachuca native plant. So here we were—a butt-head, a beak-head, and an aspiring bot-head—headed up a canyon that promised to deliver butterflies, birds, and plants.

Not far after the metalmark hitchhiked on our hood, Lynn asked which flowers were on my list for the day. "Well," I said, "as you know, I don't *really* work off a list, but I would like to see Arizona blue curls (*Trichostema arizonicum*) and the Mexican thistle (*Eryngium heterophyllum*) that grow up here, and whatever else you think is fun." For reference, we were carrying the *Provisional Flora of Garden Canyon* (eight pages, two columns,

A hawk moth visits a Mexican star thistle bloom in Garden Canyon.

small type), and the variety and selection of plants contained therein was staggering. Already we were driving past four-foot-tall icy-blue Arizona cypress (*Cupressus arizonica*) that looked like silvery Christmas trees, and the grasses were wonderfully high and lush. With little notice, Lynn piped up from the back, "Wait, wait, wait ... Turn here!" Jim swung the Explorer up a little right-hand fork until we stopped for a bathroom break. Just off the road, growing from clumps of sideoats grama (*Bouteloua curtipendula*) grass, was Arizona blue curls (*Trichostema arizonicum*), a rare two-toned white and blue flower that I had admired in photos. The royal-blue lower-petal landing pad is there to draw the pollinators in, but the most fun feature is the gracefully arching stamens, which curve over the flower like a fishing pole with a ten-pound catfish on the line. The hair-like stamens are not just there for decoration; their business is to dab pollen on the backs of visiting insects.

Up the road a little farther, Lynn said, "Over here is where that zinnia is." We pulled off, and sure enough, right where Lynn pointed on a steep slope was *Zinnia multiflora*, which to my eyes looked conspicuously like a smaller version of Grandma's annual garden zinnias. I am always interested to see the ancestors of highly bred plants, and this little pinky-red composite sure looked like the beginnings of the big floppy-headed garden zinnias. I wondered if it was a tough plant? I vaguely remembered a correspondence with Petey Mesquitey (aka Peter Gierlach) regarding it. Petey, the famed horticulturist/troubadour who often roams the southeastern Arizona grasslands *sans ropa* (that's naked, for the non-French-Spanglish speaking), had weighed in regarding this plant. I later found his e-mail message that confirmed that this wild plant was indeed vigorous in gardens:

Hello! It's *Zinnia multiflora*.....some say *Z. peruviana*.

Once you have had one or two you have it for life, at least out here. I had a bunch of seed from the Sonoita/Patagonia area that took over.

With Petey's endorsement, this zinnia seemed like a logical choice for including in Arizona gardens.

As I was setting up for pictures, I nearly plunked a leg of my tripod down on a sparkling little silver fern, which after later conferring with Russ Buhrow of Tohono Chul Park, I determined was silver star fern (*Astrolepis integerrima*). Russ, a wonderful desert-plant fanatic, is always three steps ahead of everyone else in town when it comes to growing little-noticed and hard-to-grow native desert plants. In fact, desert ferns had become one of Russ's specialties, and shortly after our Huachuca trip, I learned that Russ had grown an entire collection of desert ferns as the featured plants at Tohono Chul Park's annual fall plant sale. I had waited in line before the gates opened so as not to be left empty-fern-handed. Russ was even selling some little magic "fernrock"—a vial of white dust that approximated the limestoney conditions that these ferns prefer. So passionate was Russ about his latest fern fetish, I began to think of him as "desert fern man." Russ reported that these ferns were growing well in straight hardpan caliche (a rock-hard chalky soil substrate that plagues many desert gardens). This, I thought, is a caliche solution that is sure to surprise my garden-design clients: "Yes, Mrs. Jones, I *am* proposing that we grow ferns in your caliche!"

Jim piloted the Explorer up the rutted dirt road, which in places was a running stream of clear water from recent storms. Occasionally, we would slow down and Jim would say, "Ooo, Ooo, a red-spotted purple just came down on the road," or "There's a variegated fritillary," or "Look at the Arizona sister" or "That is a tailed orange, a summer migrant." At one point in the trip, Jim remarked that "Garden Canyon has more butterfly species than anywhere in the U.S. The count is now pushing 150." A few minutes later he added, "That's off the record; if I say that, someone may know some little canyon with a few more species, but Garden Canyon is up there." In either case, there were more—and more varied—butterflies than I could ever remember seeing anywhere. Even so, the butterflies were competing with the plants for my attention, and the plants were blowing me away. We had climbed up into the oaks and next to the road were the largest mountain mahoganies I had ever seen, lining the road. I excitedly mentioned this to Jim and Lynn, who, nonplussed, said, "Oh, those, yeah they are all over here."

We pulled over and hiked a ways up a rocky little canyon, where I found an enormous clump of Huachuca agave (*Agave parryi* var. *huachucensis*) with a strange black bug shadow-dancing on its leaf margin. We stopped for the big, flowered, fuzzy, mop-headed Mexican star thistle (*Centaurea rothrockii*), a Jupiter's beard relative that was driving the dull firetip butterflies mad. Around the bend, we finally spotted my pointed Mexican thistle, whose bracts and flowers were a haunting white barely tinged with blue. Although the Mex-

ican star thistle and Mexican thistle share similar common names, they could hardly look more different; the star thistle—feminine, flouncy, and pink—looks nothing like the Mexican thistle, whose stiff, architectural buds barely look like flowers. On a rocky cliff, coral bells (*Heuchera sanguinea*) sent up their namesake bells. When we arrived on top, I found more Huachuca agave and a mesmerizing blue penstemon with skinny leaves, which I prefer to call shoestring penstemon (*Penstemon stenophyllus*), because it shares its species name with the Australian shoestring acacia.

We ate a little lunch in the shade of oak trees. Although we hadn't done much hiking—mostly just in-and-out of the car—our little cache of sandwiches, dried apricots, and nutty Dubliner Irish cheese was rapidly gobbled up.

Up at the top, the grasses became prevalent, and since it was fall they were in their full plumage of seed heads. Jim, expert about the relationship between butterflies and grasses, explained that "females of Nabokov's satyr lay eggs on the pinyon rice grass (*Piptochaetium fimbriatum*), probably because it's easier for the first-stage caterpillars to eat. Then they move to bulb panicum (*Panicum bulbosum*), which is nearby, to finish their fall feeding before going into diapause (a period of non-feeding in the winter). The bulb panicum is a fall grass and doesn't emerge until the following summer, but the caterpillars, upon breaking diapause in the spring, have to find some grass to eat, and that is the bull grass."

"So," I chimed in, "pinyon rice grass is butterfly baby food?"

"Exactly," said Jim.

From my garden-design perspective, I admired the low green tufts of pinyon rice grass growing in

Mexican star thistle.

the shadows of alligator junipers (*Juniperus deppeana*), and the wonderful loose rosy-purple spires of bull grass (*Muhlenbergia emersleyi*), which was already available in the Arizona nursery trade with the fun cultivar name, 'El Toro'. Valuable to gardeners for the same reason it is to butterflies, bull grass begins growing its long blue-green leaves early in the spring when other ornamental grasses are still dormant. I also noticed that one of my all-time favorite grasses for desert gardens, deer grass (*Muhlenbergia rigens*), seemed to grow in wetter microclimates than the equally handsome bull grass. In some cases, perhaps because of the

wet summer, the deer grass was growing in water, while the bull grass was up on slightly drier slopes. I made a mental note to include more bull grass in my next design projects.

Before we left the grove of alligator junipers and pinyon rice grass, beak-head deftly raised her binoculars and identified a painted redstart in a high branch, just by the sound of its call. The redstart, predominantly black with a red breast, was a flashy warbler with a melodic song that went something like "warble, weacher, weacher, weacher chee." Seeing this flash of red among the green of the rice grass and junipers was a treat, and

Alligator juniper and pinyon rice grass.

I was glad we had Lynn with us to find it. When I got home I looked up the painted redstart's range and learned that it is a only a summer visitor in a few places in extreme southern Texas, New Mexico, and Arizona, and that the only place in the U.S. that they nest year-round is in some of Arizona's Sky Islands. With butt-head spouting butterfly names a mile a minute and beak-head naming both birds *and* plants, I—a humbled and a little out-of-his-element bot-head—felt lucky to be on this trip. I was soaking it all in.

On a muddy dirt road at the top of the mountain, Jim suddenly went prostrate to photograph what he pointed out was an endemic species to the Huachucas, a Huachuca giant-skipper. While Jim was trying to snap the shot, it lighted on his hand—"for the salt," he explained, as I took a picture of the butterfly.

My photographic technique, honed on more inanimate botanical objects, was abjectly poor when it came to butterflies. As gently as they could, Lynn and Jim coaxed me to "go a little slower," because my first reaction was to run, camera in hand, toward anything with colored wings. Finally, as I scared a perfect Arizona sister off of a rock while Jim was focusing on it, he remarked, "They do have eyes, you know." I wasn't very successful at the slow approach; with plants, I was often in a hurry, worrying that the light might change, the wind could kick up, the flowers would fade, and I would miss the shot. These factors considered, I rushed toward beauty.

On the dirt road coming down out of the canyon, we saw Virginia creeper (*Parthenocissus vitacea*) and bigtooth maples (*Acer grandidentatum*) beginning their progression toward red fall leaves. How wonderful, I thought, to live in a warm

desert in which, less than one hour from my home, I can be transported to a land of oaks, maples, and creeping red vines—things not usually associated with the Grand Canyon State.

On the way home, we stopped at a gas station and convenience store called G.I. Joe's that proudly displayed two armed mannequins dressed in camouflage flanking each side of the main entry. The selection of drinks was merchandised below a "Beverage Brigade" sign. Since much of Garden Canyon lies within the bounds of the Army's Fort Huachuca, it wasn't a shock to find a quicky mart with a regimental theme in the

Miraculously, the author captures a photo of an Arizona sister butterfly.

vicinity of the base. Unfortunately, this military-themed grocery didn't have one particular brand of cookie/ice cream sandwich that Jim was after, so we made a second stop. The Nestlé Toll House chocolate-chip cookie sandwiches with vanilla ice cream did top off a fine day of wildflowering.

On the drive back into Tucson, I mentioned to Jim and Lynn that this was my last trip for *Chasing Wildflowers* and that frankly, I felt a little sad about it. I had seen so much—but to be sure, I felt a little disconnected at home. I looked out the window at the golden heart-shaped leaves of cottonwood trees down in the Cienega, which reminded me of my daughter, Zoë, whose high school was also named Cienega, after this very place. Soon, I would be driving out to watch her play volleyball, a proud father, and on the way back from one of her games, if I had just enough time, and if the ocotillos were changing color and there were a few magenta-tinged sunset clouds floating in just the right places, perhaps I could take a picture or two.

Plants to find

alligator juniper *(Juniperus deppeana)*
Arizona blue curls *(Trichostema arizonicum)*
Arizona cypress *(Cupressus arizonica)*
bigtooth maples *(Acer grandidentatum)*
bull grass *(Muhlenbergia emersleyi)*
bulb panicum *(Panicum bulbosum)*
coral bells *(Heuchera sanquinea)*
deer grass *(Muhlenbergia rigens)*
Huachuca agave *(Agave parryi var. huachucensis)*
Mexican star thistle *(Centaurea rothrockii)*
Mexican thistle *(Eryngium heterophyllum)*
mountain mahogany *(Cercocarpus montanus)*

pinyon rice grass *(Piptochaetium fimbriatum)*
shoestring penstemon *(Penstemon stenophyllus)*
sideoats grama *(Bouteloua curtipendula)*
silver star fern *(Astrolepis integerrima)*
Virginia creeper *(Parthenocissus vitacea)*
wild zinnia *(Zinnia multiflora or Zinnia peruviana)*

Where to stay

Beatty's Miller Canyon Guest Ranch & Orchard
Long known to locals as a source of pesticide-free apples, eggs, honey, and beeswax, the orchard has become the hottest hummingbird-watching spot in Arizona. It's also close to much of the best Huachuca plant hunting and hiking. Be prepared to rub elbows with hummingbird-obsessed birders here.
2173 Miller Canyon Road
Hereford, Arizona 85615
520-378-2728

Where to eat

Kim Ba-Woo's Den
Thanks to Fort Huachuca and the romantic efforts of some American soldiers during the Korean War, Sierra Vista has become a stronghold for great Korean food.
1232 East Fry Boulevard
Sierra Vista, Arizona
520-459-5029

What to read

Arizona's Best Wildflower Hikes: The High Country, by Christine Maxa. Westcliffe Publishers, 2002.
Caterpillars of the Field and Garden, by Tom Allen and Jim Brock. Oxford University Press, 2005.
Hummingbirds of the American West, by Lynn Hassler Kaufman. Rio Nuevo Publishers, 2002.
Butterflies of Arizona: A Photographic Guide, by Bob Stewart. West Coast Lady Press, 2001.

Afterword

COME SPRING, I expect to be tempted by wild-flowers once again. I think about the inexhaustible options for future hunts—how much left there is to discover. Although I traveled through New Mexico twice, I missed the great clusters of claret cup cactus and yuccas blooming at White Sands National Monument. I'd like to see Ajo lilies and sand verbena in Anza Borrego in California and head back down to Baja to see what kind of floral display this year's hurricanes have stimulated. Just up the road from Tucson, Picacho Peak's Mexican gold poppies beckon. My eyes are still hungry for color.

My life on the wildflower highway has deeply informed my little garden-design practice and the way I see the world. I've begun to think that seeds are the missing link in Southwest gardens, seasonally knitting together trees, shrubs, cacti, and succulents while concealing and then revealing rock ground covers, depending on rainfall patterns. Consider this: half of the Sonoran Desert's plants are annual species. Annual plants (which most desert wildflowers are) are perfectly adapted to our desert conditions. The seeds, which can sit dormant but viable for decades, are extremely resistant to the variables of the desert climate and will wait until conditions are right to germinate. I'm not suggesting that we use copious amounts of water to trigger mass germination and bloom every year, but rather that we let the seeds go through their normal cycles of dormancy, reinvigoration (aka germination), and bloom, based on rainfall—creating exciting times in the garden when we have a wet year and quiet times during drought.

The success of a wildflower aesthetic thus depends on our acceptance of a different Western garden model that embraces brown as well as green, allowing for some space between plants, and one that, like Zen gardens, focuses on the forms of nature rather than striving for constant color and greenery. Wallace Stegner said it best: "To appreciate nature in the arid West, you have to get over the color green; you have to quit associating beauty with gardens and lawns." Perhaps more than anything, gardening with seeds requires patience; the seeds are certainly patient enough—are we?

Besides the invaluable garden-design and plant knowledge I picked up on the highway, I learned an awful lot about myself. Taking a tip from the seeds themselves, I learned to be a little less of a control freak—to use the cliché, to grow where I was planted. For me, I was planted in a life full of letters, trails, photos, plants, seeds, and drawings. I felt as though I had found my niche, and I was as happy as a Mexican gold poppy on a rocky slope. The quest for a full life, like an adventure on the wildflower highway, was full of erratic turns, unpredictability, and startling joy. In the fall of 2006, I came home and let things settle—enjoying the pleasure of having breakfast with my daughter, swimming in a cold pool, cooking apple pies with my wife, and doing my best to pay close attention to it all.

Appendix A: Tips for Wildflower Chasers

The makings of a big boomer of a wildflower spring boil down to rainfall and temperature. In the Sonoran Desert, for example, a fall that is wetter than normal and earlier than normal is a good recipe for wildflower bliss the following spring. Spring flowers need the relative warmth of the cooler months combined with moisture between September and early December. Mark Dimmitt, in *A Natural History of the Sonoran Desert*, puts it this way: "During this window, there must be soaking rains of at least one inch to induce mass germination... If the subsequent rainfall is sparse, the plants remain small and may produce only a single flower and a few seeds, but this is enough to ensure a future generation." Russ Buhrow of Tohono Chul Park speculates that we need between three and six inches over the winter to have good fall blooms, but adds, "Ten inches would be better if we want something really spectacular." Buhrow says that temperatures also influence which types of flowers will germinate: "For poppies, the ideal is a high temperature of 80 and a low of 50, along with rainfall. For owl's clover, it's more like 70 and 40, or 60 and 30."

In the Mojave Desert, rains can come later in the winter and spring and still produce vibrant displays, especially in the higher-elevation locations; along the Arizona Strip and in southern Utah, snowfall plays a role. Whatever the year, it is important to remember that there are flowers blooming *somewhere* in the Southwest for much of the year, because rainfall is often highly localized and unpredictable. For the alpine locations, wildflowers appear much later in the summer, usually July through September, but precipitation also plays a role. Luckily, the Internet has made the process of determining what's blooming, and when, a lot easier. Use these sites, which offer first-hand accounts and photos, to chart your course:

For the Greater Southwest

Desert USA (the most comprehensive wildflower site for the Southwest, even covering northern Sonora and Chihuahua, Mexico, sometimes)
www.desertusa.com

Forest Service Wildflower and Fall Foliage Hotline (a national number that also services the Southwest)
800-354-4595

Photo Travel (a website with useful links to tours, locations, and bloom info across the U.S.)
http://phototravel.com/wildflower/wf_spring.htm

For Arizona

Arizona-Sonora Desert Museum (moderated by Mark Dimmitt's wise comments, complete with yearly wildflower forecasts, this site primarily focuses on wildflower events around Tucson; includes a great list of related links)
www.desertmuseum.org/programs/flw_blooming.html

Arizona State Parks Wildflower Hotline (active during the spring months and covers most of Arizona)
602-542-4988

Boyce Thompson Arboretum
http://ag.arizona.edu/bta/events/wildflowers.html

Desert Botanical Garden (hotline is open March and April), 480-481-8134
www.dbg.org/

For California

Antelope Valley California Poppy Reserve, 661-724-1180

www.parks.ca.gov/?page_id=627

Anza-Borrego Desert State Park

www.anzaborrego.statepark.org/wildflowers.html

Carol Leigh's California Wildflower Hotsheet

http://calphoto.com/wflower.htm

Joshua Tree National Park (information about Joshua Tree and the Mojave Desert)

www.nps.gov/jotr/

Theodore Payne Foundation, southern California, phone hotline (818-768-3533) is manned only during March through May

www.theodorepayne.org/

For Colorado and northern New Mexico

Southwest Colorado Wildflowers Good info on where to find and how to photograph wildflowers in the four corners area including northern New Mexico.

www.swcoloradowildflowers.com

For more New Mexico sites

Also see the websites already listed for the Greater Southwest.

For Utah

Red Butte Gardens This sharp website with a clickable map covers the broad variety of Utah wildflowers that can be found from 2,200 feet above sea level, near St. George, to above the timberline in the Uinta Mountains at 13,500 feet.

www.redbuttegarden.org/gardening/?c=wildflower_hotline.inc

For Texas

Wild About Texas Wildflowers This unique site, with photos submitted by the Texas Department of Transportation, is clear evidence of the democratization of wildflower hunting and is a great resource for Texas.

www.lone-star.net/wildflowers/index.html

Appendix B: Tips on Growing Desert Wildflowers—Fall Sowing for Spring Bloom (for most warm areas of the Southwest)

How to plant Late September to early December is the best time to sow spring-blooming desert wildflower seeds. Work your soil with a hard rake or shovel to a depth of 4–6 inches. If hardpan soil makes tilling a large area impractical, consider using the pointed side of a digging bar to dimple the ground, creating little craters where seeds can take root. Make sure your planting area is free of weeds, and distribute seed evenly over the soil surface. Since most desert wildflowers thrive in lean, alkaline soils, soil amendments are generally not necessary. If your yard is mulched with decomposed granite, rake the seeds into the top 1/4 inch of the granite. If you have a gravel surface with spaces between the rocks, simply scatter the seeds on the surface and water them until they fall into little germinating niches between the gravel.

Watering Timing your watering to coincide with incoming wet winter storms is the best way to ensure good germination and prolonged flowering. If regular fall rains are not forthcoming, you can increase your rate of germination by watering your seeds 3 times a week for about 4–6 weeks or until seedlings appear. Once seedlings appear, a weekly watering (if it doesn't rain) will ensure good flowering. If you rely on rainfall alone, some years will be good, while other years you could end up with little or nothing, which might be just fine with you—it's your choice.

Appendix C: *Seed Collecting*

Collecting seed to store When you want to get seed from your own garden, the first question you have to answer is do you want to pick it to store it or store it in the ground. If you are picking to store, follow these recommendations:

Make sure the seed is mature. For spring-blooming flowers in the desert, seeds usually mature in May or June. When seeds are ripe they turn a dark color and become opaque. If the seed is green and wet inside, it is not ready for harvest.

Store seeds in paper bags. Plastic bags often trap moisture inside causing seeds to mold.

Keep your seeds in "human" conditions. That is, in a temperature range that humans enjoy, not too hot.

Seed banking in the ground Another method of using desert seeds is to build up a seed bank in your soil. This can be accomplished by mowing down your seed heads after they are ripe and leaving them on the ground where seeds will germinate the following year.

Some precautions Some people are allergic to some wild plant stems and/or seeds. If you are unsure about your tolerance, wear a dust mask and gloves. As Rita Jo Anthony of Wild Seed says, "collecting seed is a dirty, nasty, heavy process."

Check local regulations, but in general, never pick seed in designated wilderness areas, national parks, state parks, or on state trust land.

Roadsides and friends' yards (with their permission) are generally fair game. Exchanging seeds with friends can be a fun way to share your favorite desert plants.

Buying seed Obtaining wildflower seed from reputable vendors is the easiest way to start gardening with seeds. Buy from local companies. Clever companies who sell "wildflower meadow" mixes are unlikely to know what is native and works well in your area. Buy seed that has been collected as close to your home as possible. Check with your state's Native Plant Society for recommendations or begin with the companies listed here:

Arizona Seed Sources
Native Seeds/SEARCH
526 North 4th Avenue (retail outlet)
Tucson, Arizona
520-622-5561
www.nativeseeds.org (catalog orders)

Southwestern Native Seeds
P.O. Box 50503
Tucson, Arizona 85703
www.southwesternnativeseeds.com

Wildseed
6615 South 28th Street (mail order only)
Phoenix, Arizona 85042
602-276-3536

California Seed Sources

Seedhunt
P.O. Box 96
Freedom, California 95019-0096
www.seedhunt.com

S&S Seeds Inc.
P.O. Box 1275
Carpinteria, California 93014-1275
805-684-0436
www.ssseeds.com

Theodore Payne Foundation
www.theodorepayne.org/

Colorado Seed Sources

Pawnee Buttes Seed Inc.
P.O. Box 100
605 25th Street
Greeley, Colorado 80632
800-782-5947
www.pawneebuttesseed.com

Western Native Seed
P.O. Box 188
Coaldale, Colorado 81222
719-942-3935
www.westernnativeseed.com

New Mexico Seed Sources

Plants of the Southwest
3095 Agua Fria Road
Santa Fe, New Mexico 87507
800-788-7333
www.plantsofthesouthwest.com

Texas Seed Sources

Native American Seed
Junction, Texas
800-728-4043
www.seedsource.com

Utah Seed Sources

Desert Petals Native Seeds
P.O. Box 355
Eureka, Utah 84728
435-433-6924

Wildflowers Unlimited
P.O. Box 2114
Hildale, Utah 84784
435-616-1175
www.wildflowersunltd.com

Index

Page numbers in boldface indicate photographs.

Rio Nuevo Publishers®
P.O. Box 5250, Tucson, Arizona 85703-0250
Rio Nuevo Publishers®
P.O. Box 5250, Tucson, Arizona 85703-0250

*Pictured on pages 2-3: the maroon form of Mexican hat; page 4 (lower right): the papery seed heads of the boojum; page
5: goldfields and California poppies in Antelope Valley, California*

Library of Congress Cataloging-in-Publication Data

Calhoun, Scott.
Chasing wildflowers : a mad search for wild gardens / Scott Calhoun.
 p. cm.
Includes index.
ISBN-13: 978-1-887896-98-6
ISBN-10: 1-887896-98-8
1. Wild flower gardening—West (U.S.) 2. Wild flowers—West (U.S.) 3.
Desert plants—West (U.S.) I. Title.
SB439.24.W47C35 2007
635.9'6760978—dc22
                    2006034978

Design: Karen Schober, Seattle, Washington

Printed in Korea.

10 9 8 7 6 5 4 3 2 1